MW00715230

Did

Everything

But

Think

Did
Everything
But
Think

By

Joseph Lorick

Copyright © 2012 by Joseph A Lorick
All rights reserved. This book or any portion thereof
may not be reproduced or used in any manner whatsoever
without the express written permission of the publisher
except for the use of brief quotations in a book review.

Printed in the United States of America

First Printing, 2012

ISBN-13: 978-0615637747
(Agape Christian Books Gifts & Music)
ISBN-10: 0615637744

All Inquiries can be sent to:

8101 Harford Rd
Parkville, MD 21234
www.cocagapebooks.com
Jlor0825@gmail.com

AKNOWLEDGEMENTS

First and foremost I would like to thank God for inspiring me to overcome my own faults. I also thank my parents, who made it possible for me to overcome my environment and taught me so much about life. Without them I would be nothing. I thank my wife for her inspiration and constant support. There hasn't been anyone more affected by this process and I am so grateful for the patience she has for my non-sense. I love you, Rachelle. I thank my church family for their support and encouragement. I thank everyone that took time to read over my first draft to help me become a better writer. Lastly, I thank my Aunt Rita. She did something for me that I can never forget. My aunt took time out of her day to teach me the value of reading. When I was a toddler my aunt would take me and all the neighborhood children to Enoch Pratt Free Library. She made us check out at least one book and attend weekly story sessions. This was a rare in the middle of Baltimore City. During a time when many adults were abandoning their children to the streets, she chose a different path. Every neighborhood needs an Aunt Rita and I am so grateful she is apart my life. This book is dedicated to her and the love she shared with all the children she knew. I love you, Aunt Rita.

CONTENTS

1

WHY READ ANOTHER FINANCE BOOK

For far too long we have been influenced to lead a lifestyle that weakens financial freedom. I decided to write this book because I saw a need for more financial and socially relevant literature. We have enough investment books. I wanted to write something that truly assists all people with removing financial burdens. My goal is to empower people by providing information about lifestyle choices not consumed by debt.

I do not come from a wealthy family, but I was raised in a financially responsible household. I also grew up in one of the most financially divided cities in the U.S. Living there exposed me to the reality of a divided society. The city I am speaking of is Baltimore. Poor neighborhoods and well off neighborhoods were within blocks of each other, but never overlapped. Anyone visiting Baltimore can drive down Pratt Street and observe the differences in living standards. The areas close to the downtown are nice and further away isn't so nice. A short drive down MLK Blvd would also display similar living standards. It is as if there are two cities inside of one; a wealthy city and a poor city. People I grew up with seemed to always be struggling to overcome poverty. They were constantly trying to catch up to the living standards of well off communities. While the people I worked with always seemed to be expanding their personal empire. Many of these people never experienced financial hardship. This difference was not an absolute, but occurred more often than not. Not all people living in wealthy neighborhoods achieve financial freedom and not all people living in poor neighborhoods are broke. But the opposite is often true. The difference between achieving financial freedom and living with debt problems start with the availability of effective resources. The disparity in resources available for understanding our economy is massive and all changes need to begin here.

After working in finance over 8 years I want to share some helpful tips to avoid debt problems. I've heard countless stories of financial ruin and financial freedom. Those who were in financial ruin lacked residual income and had extremely high levels of debt. Contrary to popular belief, these people did not always earn low wages. Many people with six figure salaries have debt problems too. Financial freedom occurs when there is no dependency of loans and debt to sustain a lifestyle. The most glaring observation I made during these encounters was a lack of communication. There was always an extreme disconnect between people with debt problems and those who achieved financial freedom. Each group made assumptions about the other, but neither took time to learn from each other. A lack of communication and sharing with people outside of our community contributes to greater financial division in this society. Some people prefer this division and I am not here to bash them. Everyone has a right to their opinion. As a Christian, I believe in the principle of loving your neighbor and helping whenever possible. I prefer to give all people the information necessary to achieve financial freedom. The nation is stronger when less people are hurting.

We've become dependent of businesses that are not concerned with our well-being. The modern business model is solely about profit and pleasing investors. The aftermath of this irresponsible behavior was "The Great Recession". This recession was a part of our society from 2008 until 2011. Some of us are still in this recession. What helped to spur this recession? Lenders and marketers encouraged consumers to live a lifestyle filled with debt.

Homes were overpriced to encourage higher mortgage loans. College tuition rose and attaining a degree became difficult to earn without student loans. The newest cars were priced to require assistance from banks. All of these changes occurred overtime. Some people believe this began when the Federal Reserve was created. Others, when banks made it easier to qualify for loans. Some will point to other significant event in our history. But the government did not do this alone. Our economy is based on consumers buying into debt consumption. Persuading consumers to buy into these bad habits takes time. This process was cultivated over many years. Senior citizens can easily reveal how much our country has changed over the past 50 years. They would tell us about times when people balked at the idea of using a credit card, getting a 30 year mortgages, using car loans and building irresponsible debt. We would hear stories of families working together to overcome poverty and starting family businesses. It is easy to pick up a history book and read about the history of our economy. But the most revealing stories come from real people and not reproduced textbooks. It is unwise for us to seek answers from the very people that profit from our debt problems. These business professionals love our complacency. They make more money when we don't change. The same people producing textbooks and providing educational material are often profiting from our dependence on debt. I won't name any of these culprits, but I encourage researching textbook producers. Pay special attention to their source of funding and investors. This research will likely lead you to one conclusion. We must move beyond the stories told in these textbooks and march towards new resources for useful information.

WHY READ ANOTHER FINANCE BOOK

2

PREVIOUS GENERATIONS

B efore we expose the tools needed for financial freedom we must understand how our country became addicted to debt. The first thing to remember when looking back at history is that nothing happens over night. We could study cultures from thousands of years ago and find the footprints of our economy. Ancient Roman or Egyptian societies provide plenty information leading to the foundation of modern civilization. To avoid creating another book we will focus on certain events that contributed to the birth of American debt consumption. I will begin with the moment our country began printing money without the complete backing of gold and silver. All U.S. currency was back by gold and silver by 1861. This system was known as the gold standard. It also became the model for most established nations internationally. An oncoming war would change everything.

The cost of the Civil war prompted government leaders to temporarily leave the gold standard monetary system. This resulted in a long period of inflation. The war affected each state differently and when the U.S. returned to the gold standard it became nearly impossible to estimate the value of goods in each state. War leading to recklessness seems to be a reoccurring problem our country. The next period of time the U.S. would leave the gold standard was during World War I. We returned to the gold standard at the conclusion of the war, but the system was no longer completely balanced. There was no way to account for all currency in circulation. The Great Depression and World War II caused further harm to the system. The Federal Reserve chose to print more money, backed by nothing but trust, to cover national debts. Wars are not cheap and the U.S. will strive to win at any cost. Following World War II the U.S. did have an opportunity to return to a gold based system. We increased our gold supply from international seizures, but did not use it to completely back currency. Government leaders had something else in mind. The Bretton Wood agreement made the U.S. dollar the dominant world reserve currency. This was based on American political pressure on foreign nations and our massive gold supply. With this new power the U.S. and Federal Reserve started printing more dollars than our gold reserve and some countries became aware of this practice. This caused France and other countries to demand gold in exchange for the currency they held in the late 1960's. As a result the U.S. gold supply decreased and a few years later President Nixon stop meeting countries request for gold. After these events the dollar became more of an accepted value instead of a promissory note backed by real assets. The value of the dollar decreased and as U.S. consumption grew so did the national debt level.

Monetary systems like the one we have today contributed to the downfall of many other nations and empires. The fall of the Roman Empire is one example. Placing more money with no backing in circulation to address the national debt problems will usually cause long term debt problems. Somehow our government never learned this lesson. Politicians seem to like the idea of creating national debt problems. The government was not alone in creating this dependency of debt; banks and lenders helped too.

Bank lending practices and gradual changes in usury laws contributed to our debt culture. Usury laws protect people and businesses from paying excessive interest on loans. The principle of usury can be dated back to Old Testament biblical writings from Moses to the Jews. Back then, lending to another Jewish person for gain was unlawful. Foreigners did provide an exception to this law, but it was rarely used. The early Christian churches also considered lending for gain to be sinful. Christianity was quickly becoming the most popular religion in Europe. This expansion of Christian beliefs presented a problem for many lenders. The only people willing to lend with interest were Jews and this limited opportunities to open banks. This is why most international banks were often owned by Jewish families. It also helps to explain how the banking industry is setup today. Take a look at the history of the chairman of the Federal Reserve you will find an interesting cultural trend. Banks provided much needed income for many European countries and usury laws began to be minimalized. It may have begun with government approval, but most citizens began to adapt to lending with interest. This change did have many opponents. Aristotle, Karl Marx, Plato and John Maynard Keynes are just a few. Despite their efforts this practice became a part of modern European civilizations. The United States followed a similar path. Once states were established in the U.S. usury laws were created. By 1915, most states created usury statues without interference from the federal government and bankers were often prosecuted for usurious loans. These usury criminals were viewed by many as the lowest people in society and not tolerated in local communities. People viewed personal loans as unnecessary and often avoided loans at all cost. People began to change their minds as the economy began to shrink. Loans were often the only method of avoiding poverty. But, banks decreased lending as defaults increased. People started to panic as the economy fell into a terrible recession. Thousands lost their jobs. Rumors of an economic collapse started to spread and people lost their faith in banks. Banks were required to keep 10% of their money in reserves and when people began to clear out their accounts, banks ran out of money. The Great Depression officially arrived and banks were failing by the thousands. This event ruined the reputation of banks and lending began to decline. People preferred to move on without using financial institutions. They didn't want to risk their hard earned money. It took decades to change this perception, but in the late 1940's a few gentlemen had an idea that would change lending forever. Frank McNamara, Ralph Schneider and Alfred Bloomingdale came up with the idea of using a card for temporary loans. They would charge small fees and interest for using the card. Today, we call this a credit card. There were individual merchant credit cards available before this event took place, but this card could be used at multiple businesses. These cards were only offered to people with proven wealth. This new way of lending appeared to be better than standard loans. People always want to be a part of something exclusive and eventually this desire led to the explosion of this industry. Within the next 20 years more credit card companies were started. Merchants began to regularly accept credit cards as a form of payment and the economy was booming. These combinations of events contributed to the growth of the credit card industry, but many states usury laws would limit its early success. This would all change in 1978 .The Marquette Supreme Court ruled in favor of nationally chartered banks. Banks could charge the interest rates allowed in their headquarters state anywhere. This effectively destroyed state usury laws and led most banks to move their headquarters to states with the highest interest lending limits. Credit Card companies did not reap the rewards of this ruling until the mid to late 1980's. This period of time represented the largest percentage increase of credit card use ever. The economy had come out of a short recession and spending was prevalent. Having a credit card made it easier for people to obtain their desires. With the economy growing and spending rising the media industry saw an opportunity to make more money.

Televisions were in almost every household by the 1980's. Marketing executives could reach millions of consumers through one channel. Ideals of rich and glamorous lifestyles and acquiring the newest gadgets were spreading at an unstoppable pace. People from all income levels were affected. Marketers reached consumers quicker and more efficient than ever before. The opportunity to influence consumers buying habits on a wide scale was too tempting to remain socially responsible. Adults in their 20's and 30's increased their debt more than ever before. Their actions would not go unnoticed by their children. They were being raised to believe this behavior was normal. Previous generations grew up with a different concept of personal finance. They lived through the Great Depression and during a time when fiscal responsibility was a priority. This generation wasn't prepared for this level of advertising. A mixture of television ads, radio ads and newspaper ads used to reach all consumers. Shows like "Lifestyle of the Rich and Famous (1984-1995), The Oprah Winfrey Show (1986-2011), Entertainment Tonight (1981-present), and many more brought viewers closer to celebrities than ever before. This exposure helped create a strong desire to acquire a lifestyle beyond the average household income level. People did not know celebrities drove cars like Ferrari's Testarossa's, Lamborghini's Countach's and Rolls Royce's without the aid of television. Most communities didn't have residents that owned these vehicles. This exposure led to a desire for luxury vehicles. Used cars were no longer good enough. This exposure led to envy and covetousness behavior; which translated to increasing debt. Many adults did not know the odds of achieving this lifestyle were extremely low. An increase in television ads also contributed to influencing debt growth. Commercials occupied more television airtime than ever before. In the 1960's, an hour-long American show would only include roughly 9 minutes of commercials. The average today is about 22 minutes of advertising time to each one hour show. This drastic increase can be first observed during the 1980's. Increased media advertising, lifestyle shows and a booming economy was too tempting for most people to handle. The 1980's ushered in a new era of consumption. The people most vulnerable to this newly established debt culture can be identified by race.

There are a number of events that impacted vulnerability to this debt culture. Slavery caused all racial minorities to fall behind white Americans in all social aspects of American life. Many people want to forget this ugly part of our history, but the effects of slavery still exist today. They may never leave our society. Slaves had no rights and were regarded as property in the U.S. Constitution. It would be 340 years before minorities (particularly people of African descent) would be considered a person. Some empires are built and fall in less time. The U.S. became a free independent country and slaves never had the opportunity to be an equal investor its growth. They couldn't start large businesses or own land. When slavery was finally abolished in 1865, some slave owners ignored it. Many people continued to be held as slaves, but it did mark the beginning of the end of U.S. slavery. The end of slavery did not create equality for all U.S. citizens. Black people and other minorities had been upgraded from slaves to second class citizens. Second class citizens did not have the right to control their environment because they were unable to vote. They couldn't purchase certain homes or receive adequate legal protection. Race limited opportunities to obtain certain jobs, loans, quality education and removed many other promised rights. African Americans did not have complete equal rights in the United States. Other minority groups also experienced these inequalities, but not like black people. Outside of Native Americans, most other minorities were immigrant citizens. They weren't discriminated against as much as blacks due to their lower population numbers. Blacks were brought into this country as slaves. Some people will argue that black people still don't have complete equal rights, but I will leave that for another writer to debate. This period of legal inequality caused blacks and all other minorities to stay behind whites from a financial standpoint. Minorities were the majority of the lower income citizens in the

United States. Minorities helped build the United States infrastructure by obtaining manual labor jobs but rarely owned any companies benefiting from an ever growing economy. They were not the chief executive officers of banks or owners of large farmlands. The presidents of major corporations, owners of major construction companies and political positions belonged to white men. These were the higher paying positions. Minorities had to settle for lower paying jobs. As a result, many had to live in the poorest and most unsafe areas in the country. Police protection from criminals was not equal among all races and most blacks had to live amongst the worst criminals. Minority communities were infiltrated with drugs and broken job markets. Black men weren't present in more households than any other race in the United States. Schools did not have enough classrooms and books for their students. These living standards were terrible when compared to most whites. By the1960's laws were changed to promote equality. Black people were no longer legal considered second class citizens. The Civil Rights Act of 1960 stopped voter discrimination. The Equal Pay Act of 1963 prevented wage discrimination based on gender. The Civil Rights Act of 1964 limited the ability for any business owner, school, and voter register to discriminate based on race. The Civil Rights Act of 1968 expanded discrimination laws to housing. These laws helped to minimalize discrimination but didn't deter many business owners from practicing racism. The chances of being prosecuted for discrimination were low. It took hundreds of years for minorities to have the same rights as whites. Some people refuse to adjust their way of thinking. The government cannot force anyone to follow their laws. While these changes were occurring the majority of black Americans and other minorities still resided in the poorest communities. Good paying jobs continued to be given to whites based on race. Many black people grew tired of this environment. Some even choose to enlist in the military as an escape. Others were drafted into the military.

College student avoided the draft but many others could not. The majority of minorities happened to fall in the non-college student category. These circumstances contributed to the lack of minority integration into corporate America. African Americans made up roughly 13 percent of all soldiers enlisted in the Vietnam War while they only represented 11 percent of total U.S. population during the 1960's. They also made up a high percentage of combat and infantry soldiers during the Vietnam War. These figures eventually dropped towards the end of the war but the effects lasted much longer. The war ended in 1975 and many minority men no longer had a job. Coming back home from the war did not guarantee a job. The U.S. was experiencing a recession and many soldiers had to deal with physical and psychological issues before returning to work. These circumstances did not help minority workforce advancement. Minorities always lose the most jobs during tough economic conditions. The U.S. experienced another recession in the early 1980's and finally started to recover in the later part of 1982. In mid-1980's minorities began to become a part of corporate America in larger numbers. The jobs being offered were at the lowest levels but this still was an improvement. All of these changes coincided with the expansion of debt. Many minorities were tired of living in America's poorest communities. They wanted to experience wealth. After living in substandard environments for so long many black people craved immediate change. I was one of those people. I had those same desires and did not understand why. I didn't have wealthy grandparents, parents, aunts, uncles, cousins, and friends to learn from. I was a child surrounded by people that didn't fully understand personal finance. My parents did their best to teach me, but they couldn't explain habits they didn't know. This is the kind of environment many minorities are raised in. We live in communities more susceptible to an evolving debt culture partially due to starting from behind.

3

CHILDHOOD INFLUENCES

As a child there were only a few things that were important to me; food, toys, video games, television and just plain fun. I had no idea this country was coming out of a recession or that a few years before most household didn't have a television. I was not aware of the financial struggles my parents were experiencing, but I knew my family wasn't rich. I didn't learn this from my friends or people in the neighborhood. There were no luxury vehicles, mansions, gated communities or community centers; just row homes and small corner stores. The kids I went to school with lived with pretty similar circumstances and they didn't introduce me to the concept of wealth. My parents did not talk to me about their financial abilities. If they did speak about money it was not in front of me. I learned I was not rich or even considered poor from television. I can't say what show it was or what commercial I was watching. What I do remember is being introduced to the concept of rich and poor. I saw game shows where people won thousands of dollars and expensive vacations. I remember commercials with the newest video game systems and toys my family couldn't afford. I watched show like, "The Lifestyles of the Rich and Famous", and wondered why my family couldn't live in luxury. Television helped to shape my concept of money and many other children seemed to share the same experience. I remember one of the first games I learned to play was "That's my car"; which involved sitting on the side of a busy street and being first to claim ownership of the best looking car. I constantly told myself, "When I grow up I am going to buy my parents a mansion and get everything I want". I completely dismissed the possibility of my parents providing a wealthy lifestyle. I assumed we would always be poor. In my mind, I had to become rich to change these circumstances. This desire to be rich and wealthy started very early in my childhood. It was the birth of my misconception of wealth. The media shouldn't get all of the credit for my conception of money. There were a lot of contributors to my misunderstanding.

Friends, family, music and television are major influences in most children lives. A short conversation with a child can reveal how much these environmental factors influence their way of thinking. They learn from everything that surrounds them and this happens most often during early childhood. Despite the many difference within the environment children are raised in, they usually have similar ideas about wealth. Many children believe rich is defined as the ability to instantly obtain objects of desire; in other words being able to buy anything you want. This is where most of our debt problems and numerous financial misconceptions began. Wealth has nothing to do with quantity of materials. Adults understand how to keep up wealthy personas while suffering financially, but children don't know the difference. They can't tell who really has money and who doesn't. All children can do is look around their living environment and make judgments. The first people that are in line to be judged are parents.

Children with parents that can explain money matters and finance are usually better prepared to handle personal finances through adulthood. Children that do not gain an accurate understanding of money are often less prepared. A young child needs to be told that buying everything he or she desires is not always responsible and material items do not bring true happiness. Children need to be taught the proper way to budget money. They must learn the truth about money supply limits. Some parents do this by giving an allowance, starting a savings account, limiting gifts and being financially responsible themselves. Parents also need to practice financial responsibility to have the best impact on the financial habits of their children. The old saying, "Do as I say and not as I do", can create discipline but doesn't give children a hands on example of financial responsibility. How much did you want to do things your parents told you not to? Wasn't it worse more tempting when you saw them doing it? The urge to disobey grows stronger when parents don't practice what they preach. Another result of not teaching children good financial habits through example is a loss of respect. If parents are no longer viewed as a good resource for information then children will look elsewhere for help. Their search will often lead them to celebrities because of an attraction to wealth. Celebrities are very visible and their wealth is usually the focus of the media. This is especially true for children that are raised in middle or lower income communities. When these children don't know anyone considered rich they often go to the next best thing; rich people seen on television. Parents are on the front line in the war against debt and underestimating this responsibility often leads to long term financial problems. To keep this from happening parents must understand which factors can lead their children towards a lifestyle consumed by debt.

What children see on television becomes more influential when parents don't prepare them for what they are watching. This is one reason many children want to be famous athletes, singers, rappers, comedians and actors. When children see their favorite football player featured in a luxury car commercial they quickly lose a grasp of reality. Even if children watch children themed television channels like The Disney Channel or Nickelodeon they are still bombarded by ads featuring celebrities. These shows can be influential too. One of the most popular shows, Hannah Montana, is partially based on the life of a performer. This show may provide good life lessons but it can also create unrealistic expectations. How often does a person become a famous singer? People have a better chance at winning the lottery. These shows are dominating television airtime. They have replaced the George Jefferson's and Archie Bunkers of the world. Poor and lower middle class families are rarely represented on television. The most popular shows promote financial success and create a false perception of reality. In fact, some are called Reality T.V. shows. These shows have been around for many decades but never dominated the airwaves as they do today. It is almost impossible to go one day without hearing a conversation about these shows. They are spoken about on news reports, social networks, schools, internet sites, at the workplace and just about anywhere else people socialize. American Idol, MTV Cribs, Teen Cribs, My Super Sweet Sixteen, Celebrity Apprentice, America's Best Dance Crew, Dancing With the Stars, Top Model, Project Runway, Love And Hip Hop, Baseball Wives, Mafia Wives, What Chilli Wants, Keeping Up with the Kardashians, Kendra, Married to Rock, Fantasia For Real, Flavor of Love, Rock of Love, I Love New York, Basketball Wives, Football Wives, I Know My Kid's a Star, Celebrity Fit Club, Extreme Makeover, Pimp My Ride, Secret Millionaire, Jersey Shore, Real Housewives of ....and many more reality shows rule the television airways. People are attracted to watching the lifestyles of socialites. Reality T.V. shows give viewers the illusion of gaining insight to how celebrities live or how people become celebrities. The majority of these shows offer no true depiction of their reality. They don't explain everything necessary to attain their wealth or how rare it is to reach celebrity status. There are no cameras following the countless trips to acting or music classes, numerous failed auditions, short term financial losses, meetings with executives, hiring of agents, family setbacks, divorces and many other less glamorous parts of celebrity life. The public is not made aware of the money paid to the cast and the scripts being written for each episode. Reality T.V. is far from true reality. If children are able to avoid these shows, another distraction can come in the form of game shows. Jeopardy, Who Wants to Be a Millionaire, Survivor, Minute to Win It, Shark Tank, Wipeout, Wheel of Fortune, Are You Smarter Than a 5th Grader and many other game shows give the illusion of easy or endless money. These shows reward their contestants monetarily in exchange for successful completion of their game. Children will see people win money on television every day of the week and the effect of this repetition is a perception of easy money. Adults may know how unrealistic it is to appear on a game show but children do not. Music Videos also have a strong influence on the concept of money to children. The purpose of a music video is to build a fan base for artist that will lead to future purchases. Music videos are rarely a depiction of reality and offer many people an escape into a fantasy world. Without the help of adults; children may not understand what they are watching. They need to be told these videos are more about fantasy than reality. Very rarely do you see a video featuring poor or under privileged people as they really are. The genre of music that a music video is based on also has an effect on perception because of common themes. It's a proven fact that the majority of Hip Hop videos promote wealthy lifestyles; while most other music videos are more varied. This celebration of wealth and riches in Hip Hop music videos often causes children to interpret the theme as reality. These videos rarely offer an explanation of how wealth is attained. Even when artist try to explain how they amassed their riches through illegal means; it's still vastly exaggerated. In the real world these artist were never big time kingpin drug dealers or modern day "Tony Montana's"; they are just artist reflecting a small part of society. There is nothing wrong with celebrating success but Hip Hop could use a little more balance. Hip Hop music videos are not the only videos that misrepresent reality. All musical genre's do this because it sells. People don't want to watch videos and become depressed. Music videos assist with temporarily escaping the negative aspects of reality. They can even inspire people to reach for their dreams. But children still need to be taught how to process what they are seeing. To be fair it is not the artist responsibility to make sure children don't watch or are mentally prepared for these videos; that belongs to the parents and family. Artists have never forced anyone to watch their videos. Music videos are nothing compared to the music itself.

Music is and always will be influential in our daily lives and it can have a profound effect on children. The type of music that we enjoy in our adulthood is usually determined in our childhood. I cannot remember the first song I ever heard but I can remember when I started listening to my favorite songs. When I was 5 years old I listened to an artist named Michael Jackson. Millions of other children did too. I was young but the influence Michael Jackson had on my life just from listening to his music was unbelievable. I was dressing, dancing and singing as if I were Mike as often as I could. He was an icon in my eyes. If Mike said it was cool to drink Pepsi then I wanted a Pepsi. If he said we needed to care about poor people then I cared. When he asked "Whose Bad", I made sure to let everyone know how bad I was. Eventually, I would go on to become a fan of many other artists, but in my childhood I was truly a fan of music and the artist. When you hear that an artist sells 1 million records, more than half of those purchases were made by parents for their children. Children are the most faithful and impressionable fans of musicians because of a lack of life experiences. Musicians are telling them about a world they have never seen and showing them how anyone can be adored through music. Children love to escape reality or see beyond their current environment and music fulfills this desire. Most adults are not faithful fans like their children because of life experiences and the complexity of their lifestyles. Adults often use music to escape reality instead of allowing it to shape their perspective of reality.

CHILDHOOD INFLUENCES

Most young children don't have this ability and music can lead to misconceiving reality. The most common topics in music today are partying, sex, money and love, but for obvious reasons I will focus on money. Making a lot of money and living a wealthy lifestyle is spoken about quite often in popular music. It has become a norm to speak about wealth in music, but it's most prevalent in Hip Hop. If you take a look at the Billboard charts I am sure you will see how the top 20 of all popular songs touches money but still has some variety. The top 20 songs in Hip Hop have a lot more to do with money. These songs revolve around money but very rarely give anyone listening information that will lead to financial well being. The majority of these songs are about spending money and the power money brings a person. In these songs the goal is always to be the boss or person with the most power, but rarely do you hear these songs portray everyday blue collar workers as success stories. Buying out the bar, driving expensive cars, making it rain in the club, going on expensive vacations and other means of instant gratification are realistic for people who can afford to live this way. Those people only represent roughly 10 percent of the total U.S. population. Unfortunately, many children don't realize this. Just like when I was a fan of Michael Jackson and many other artists in my childhood; children idolize artist that produce these type of songs. Hip Hop is not the only music contributing to learning bad money habits. These types of songs exist in every genre of music. Many parents try to offset these misperceptions by teaching them about the real world, but run into trouble because they are listening to these same songs. Unlike some previous generations; today more parents and children listen to the same type of music. My parents and I didn't listen to the same type of music. We enjoyed a few songs together but my parents were not fans of hip hop. My children are more likely to listen to the same type of music I listen to. This is happening because of the longevity and popularity of pop and hip hop music. When parents try to limit their children from listening to the music they enjoy it becomes sensationalize. Children want to emulate adults and rules alone will not remove this desire. There are so many mediums for children to listen to music that parents can't possibly monitor them all. Children can listen to music on cell phones, mp3 players, laptops, desktops, radios, television and more. These circumstances create a need for parents to consistently reinforce good money principles. The other people that can help offset the influence music has on children are teachers and school administrators.

School is one of the most influential places a child will spend their conscious time. This is where they will meet friends, develop skills for their future career, learn about the world and go through many other life changing experiences. School is a place for educating children and adults. The goal is to prepared people to function in society; but not all schools accomplish this task. Teachers and administrators jobs are to educate and provide a safe learning environment for all children. The background and demographics of each child should not have any effect on this service being provided, but it does. Anyone that tries to sell people on the idea that all schools provide an equal opportunity to learn is either lying or misinformed. Overall public schools are not as good as private schools and most public schools in wealthy zip codes are better than those in low income zip codes. The reasons for this disparity vary based on the person you are asking. Some people will say it's due to funding, classism, racism, government conspiracies, politics and many other reasons. I believe it's due to selfishness. In my opinion, too many people don't care about other people and the success of future generations. We have a value problem and all of the failures in our school system are just symptoms of this problem. Many people create civil unrest to support our soldiers, gay rights, animal cruelty and labor rights; but not for the cause of education equality. Those other groups have many more active supporters. This lack of caring is what allows underachieving schools to exist and as long as this is the case, everyone must be careful when choosing how to educate their children. Many people are choosing to home school their children because of the lack of consistency between all schools. According to NCES, there were 1.5 million students identified as home schooled in the United States in 2007. This was a 74 percent increase from 1999 statistics and is even higher though 2011. School safety and curriculum is one of the top reasons parents choose home schooling over public schools. Their concerns are very legitimate. The risk of sending children to a school that doesn't provide resources necessary for success is too high to not be taken seriously. These schools don't always stand out. They don't always produce unsatisfactory test scores because all schools don't use the same testing and scoring standards. The aftermath is confusion while trying to compare education quality.

The most common way to judge the quality of schools is to look at student achievement after graduation. Schools with high graduation rates and working alumni are what I call successful schools. Unsuccessful schools by default would be the opposite. One big difference between successful schools and unsuccessful schools is the curriculum. Successful schools don't just offer basic math and reading classes. They offer classes that teach lessons about functioning in society. Instead of only requiring classes that teach math functions and arithmetic; they add classes about budgeting, lending, debt management and all other aspects of personal finance. Understanding how much change should be returned while making a purchase is not enough information to lead children on a path of financial stability. Children need to know how money circulates in our country and the effects of its misuse. Another characteristic of successful schools is a grading system that accurately displays how much children have learned. Some school systems agree that achieving at least a 60% success rate is proficient while others start at 70%. A child could get a C in both schools but would not have learned at the same level. This contributes to the disparity of quality education. Parents should not have to worry about differences in minimal achievement levels and how it affects the future abilities of their children. Scoring should be the same for all schools. Based on my counseling conversations, early childhood education is very important to long term financial freedom. Most people I had spoken with contributed some of their financial success or failure to education. The people with debt problems never attended schools that prepared them for life. This was not the sole contributing factor, but it did stand out as a common trend. On the other hand, when I spoke with people experiencing financially freedom; they would speak of learning budgeting skills in grade school. Some of their parents reinforced these principles but having this information available through schools made it easier to accept. Early childhood education stays with people throughout their adulthood; therefore, being prepared to handle finances at an early age will be the foundation for future financial decision making. If you were to ask a college student to recall lessons learned in college and then ask them to recall lesson learned in grade school; many would recall the later better. Good schools also provide students with counselors that assist with career, social and educational development. Schools with low budgets can't afford to hire a lot of counselors and some students don't get the assistance needed for success. Students learn in different manners. Teachers cannot adjust to the learning habits of every student and having counselors to back them up helps everyone. Counselors also help keep schools safer by proving additional security and having a relationship with children that can be trusted during trying times. Many students prefer the advice of counselors over teachers when dealing with personal problems. Teachers that perform counseling and teaching roles are a rarity. Those are the best teachers. School budgets limit the ability to attract these teachers. A good teacher is not responsible for raising children but will do everything possible to assure their students are well educated. Low budget school systems have a problem attracting good teachers to their schools. Why would most teachers want to work in schools offering low pay and little resources? Once again the best schools will attract the best teachers while other schools only have a few. As long as these differences exist between schools, there will not be an equal opportunity for learning. Underestimating the effect schools have on the future financial stability of all children is a huge mistake. Parents must choose carefully.

Childhood friends have a high level of influence on all children and are a necessary part of life. A childhood without friends often leads to psychological and social problems later in life; therefore, children should not go without them. This principle is true for all human beings not matter what physical and economical differences there may be. I could not imagine what my life would have been like as a child without friends and I am grateful for having had them in my life. The amount of trust and faith children put in each other is unmatched outside of parents and siblings. Children want to spend as much time as possible with their friends because of the fun. During these fun filled encounters a lot of information is being exchanged. When they share information amongst one another they often believe whatever they are being told due to a lack of life experiences. Just think back to your own childhood and recall the countless rumors, advice and other tales you were told about by a friend. Much of this information was untrue or an exaggeration of the truth; unfortunately; many of us had to find out the truth after an embarrassing experience. Friends often introduce children to a new perspective of life because they represent a set of values unique to their own household. The lessons children learn about money and wealth from their household are frequently spread between each other; just like any other part of life. Some children are taught or believe money has an endless supply and being rich means being able to buy almost anything. Other children are taught that they need to for the future or that some celebrity is the standard to measure against success. These beliefs about money and personal finance vary and are shared between children. When children brag to other children about all their games and clothes; it leaves an impression. These types of conversations happen more often than conversations about saving and this should be expected of a child. Budgeting and financial responsibility is not and should not be an attractive topic for children. I always told my friends stories about why I couldn't get something I wanted. I can recall being upset with my parents for not being able to buy me what I wanted. I responded by creating plans to become rich, so I could buy anything I wanted. I thought my parents were poor because they couldn't afford to buy me everything I wanted and they were only trying to teach me lessons about money. My parents attempted to explain why this happened, but I didn't understand until I was older. Their ability to buy me something had nothing to do with me getting what I wanted. Most of the things I wanted so badly were because my friends had it and not because I really wanted it. I can't recall how many toys and games my parents purchased ended up gathering dust 30 days later. This is a story many people can tell about their childhood. It is also another early contributor to the development of financial perceptions. I am thankful for my parents teaching me this lesson, but what about the children that don't have this resource at home? They are more susceptible to the influence of their friends and many times end up misinformed or with an inaccurate concept of money. These are the children that need a big brother or sister, guidance counselors and any other source of adults with knowledge of fiscal responsibility. Many children don't receive this type of help because adults stop caring.

We are all selfish and competitive by nature. We like to make sure our families are taken care of but will ignore our neighbors. Children are not exempt from this character trait. When the most popular kid in school or a best friend has something that another child doesn't; it often leads to a desire to obtain those things. No child wants to feel left out and the reason they feel this way is usually connected to their peers. Children make each other feel bad when one of them is lacking something everyone else has or something popular. How many times can you recall either making fun of another kid or being made fun of when you were a child? Accepting that all children will experience some level of teasing is the first step to understanding how to combat it. Most children will respond to this teasing by requesting whatever popular item everyone else has. They can create the most interesting stories to compel parents to make a purchase. Some will claim a pair of shoes will add to their learning abilities. Others will say popularity is essential to their happiness. Children need to understand that being ridiculed is normal and friends will come and go. Having this mentality will lessen the influence children have on each other. It will also help them to make better decisions when they get older. Early childhood lessons are the foundation of teenage decision making. These lessons will help determine how they respond to similar influences as a teen.

CHILDHOOD INFLUENCES

4

TEENAGE INFLUENCES

When we became teenagers something happened. It was the first period of our lives when we could use more than a decade of experiences as a basis for our decision making. We were no longer the toddlers that followed our older siblings and family members around to see what they were doing. There was a lot less doing things just because we were told to. We wanted an explanation. We had more than 10 years of observing and learning and were ready to make more decisions for ourselves. These life experiences were now a part of our decision process and we chose to rely on them or not. This is a common theme for all teens and the days of thinking like a young child ended. All teens go through this change of thinking. Young children usually make decisions based on another person's advice or example, but teens are more aware of all the choices they can make. They are more exposed than ever before and have formed judgments based on 12 years of observation. The guidance they did or did not receive during early childhood will be used in decision making. Those lacking guidance are more prone to poor decision making. This is why many teens are making bad life choices. There is a serious lack of guidance. These bad decisions will eventually lead to a difficult adulthood. Parents that prepare their young children for future life experiences will still experience difficulties, but having a foundation developed during early childhood still helps. Teens are more influenced by television, music, friends, peers and school then when they were younger. Parents need to understand these influences to best help their teen transition into adulthood.

Parents lose some influence when their children become teenagers. They are no longer the source for all answers. Competition for influence is at an all-time high. One reason that influence has weakened is because many teens are under a false perception. They believe a decade of life experiences makes them smarter than mom and dad. All parents of teenagers have witnessed this paradigm shift and it is to be expected of all children. Does the phrase, "How do you know what you are talking about when you haven't done…." sound familiar? There is always someone that has achieved a greater status in life than mom or dad and many teenagers believe those people offer great advice. I remember the countless times I questioned my parents about everything from chores to school and am thankful my parents didn't take my life for all the stress I caused. The truth is; I was only doing what they did when they were my age. Most teenagers don't realize that social achievements doesn't equate to intelligence. Everyone faces life challenges that have to be overcome and can teach from those experiences. There are many life lessons to be learned from someone that has lost everything or someone living moderate lifestyle. I learned plenty of lessons about the effects of alcohol addiction by attending AA meetings with my father. The stories I heard from people at the lowest point of their lives made it possible for me to avoid those mistakes. I didn't feel a need to learn what it is was like to be an alcoholic because they did it for me. Hearing stories about losing family members and physical abilities was enough for me. With all the changes teens are experiencing parents lose some influence over them, but still play a crucial role in their development. Losing some influence on teens creates a need for parents to fully utilize the influence they still have. Parents have to consistently reinforce good personal finance practices at this stage because inconsistency will create more doubt in their ability to teach. Teenagers are always looking for ways to disprove or disobey instructions their parents are giving; therefore, mistakes give them a way out of following directions. A parent that is spending money recklessly and creating large debts is leading their child to doom. Teenagers are observing which cars are bought. They remember the vacations parents take and the amount of jewelry purchased. They know how often parents use credit cards instead of paying in cash. All spending habits are up for review. Playing the lottery every week doesn't help either. The odds of winning millions from the lottery are very slim and when parents make the chances seem realistic they can be the early source of gambling problems. Parents must practice discipline if they want to give their children the best chance to succeed in the future. There may come a time in the future when children understand the spending habits of their parents, but as a teen it is hard to understand. Another reason parents lose some influence over their child is because of the increase of influence from television, music, school, and peers.

Teens do not watch television the same way young children do. Children network shows and cartoons are replaced by adult themed shows. The entertainment room is no longer the only room to watch television. Older children usually have a television in the bedroom. Teens watch late night television shows because they go to sleep later in the evening. This change exposes teens to commercials and shows with more adult content. Sexual performance and dating/chatting ads flood the airwaves in the late evening. Avoiding them is nearly impossible. These commercials were previously shown between 11pm and 6am. Today, they are can be seen anytime. Teenagers also become are more targeted consumer. Young children don't have the same buying power as teenagers. Teens can acquire paying jobs and maintain some level of influence on their parents purchasing habits. Why else would marketers use celebrities and teen idols to promote their products? They are aware of its effect on teens. What good business professional would ignore the benefits of this practice? Older consumers do not generate the long term income needed to expand empires. Marketers like to start grooming customers at an early age. One method they will use is to produce get rich quick infomercials. The popularity of these infomercials has significantly increased over the past 10 years. In previous years, they were broadcasted between midnight and 6 am, but now there are channels dedicated to these ads. They are dangerous to teenagers because of their misleading messages. These infomercials create an impression that it is easy to become wealthy. They tell consumers to purchase their literature or join some club to learn the secrets of financial success. Due to the effectiveness of these ads, scam artist are using them to attract new victims. The FTC is actively pursuing companies producing deceptive infomercials, but they can't catch them all. By this age, most teenagers realize it is unrealistic to win money on game shows, but infomercials are more believable. These sales pitches are not only on television but are reinforced through internet websites and bogus testimonials. Thousands of YouTube videos have been created to persuade people to join sales teams with the promise of wealth. If you think these infomercials are ineffective just ask recent college graduates about its effectiveness. I will never forget the first pyramid scheme I fell for and the disappointment it bought me. The hiring manager promised me wealth, power and success. The idea of failure was ridiculous. Their product was the best and in high demand. They told me there was no way I would not make a lot of money. When I started selling their products I quickly realized they were selling false hope. People were not asking for my products and certainly didn't need them. I couldn't blame these marketers for targeting me. I was young and gullible. I found this company online, but I see infomercials for similar companies every day. These infomercials are very misleading but aren't the most influential television programs teenagers will watch. The most enticing shows are based on entertainment.

TEENAGE INFLUENCES

Music television and reality shows have become more prevalent than ever before and most teens are highly influenced by them. These television programs offer a realistic escape from reality. No, they don't believe in the special effects used in videos, but they do believe living a wealthy lifestyle is realistic. Only a few artists make millions from their work and most don't have long careers. Not understanding or knowing this has caused teens to pursue a lifestyle that is unrealistic. The stories they hear from celebrities about overcoming poverty and eventually becoming rich through the entertainment industry are misleading. I hate to be the bearer of bad news for any teenager reading this book, but most of you will not become a rich celebrity. Reality shows have the same effect without as much glitz and glam. Most of these shows are easy for young children to avoid because of parental oversight. But once they get older these shows become the majority of what they watch. Hiding the world from teenagers is nearly impossible, so it is better to prepare them for these programs. Teenagers need to know the limitations of television. Television shows lack a complete explanation of the process necessary to become wealthy because cameras don't capture small details. Television producers have a job to entertain viewers and these small details can be boring. Producers don't make money from boring shows and will edit out informative content in favor of foolishness. If these explanations don't work, then limiting the time teenagers watch television may be necessary. Children between the ages 12 and 17 spend roughly 4 hours per day watching television. Cutting this time by at least 1 hour will significantly reduce its influence.

I love listening to music and cannot imagine life without it. Artist should have the right to express themselves in whatever manner they please. I am not in favor of them being role models. But, no matter how I or anyone else feels they are role models. The influence musicians have on people is undeniable and teens are very susceptible to it. Parents are old and outdated in the eyes of most teens. Musicians are the leaders of style and culture. They are adored by millions and what teen doesn't want to be popular? Rock stars are on the cover of magazines, in popular movies, on television shows, and have the attention of the general public. Mom and Dad are not selling out stadiums and don't have songs in the Billboard Top 100; except for the parents of the Blue Ivy or Willow Smith. The songs these popular artists perform are not influential because of talent; they give teens something they yearn for. Music allows teenagers to own something outside of their parents' possession. It helps them achieve a small level of independence. Teenagers are told to go to school, get good grades, do their chores, and follow many other rules set by adults. But their preference of music is something no adult can control. At this stage of their life independence and creating an identity is very important. Music only helps them achieve this. Popular artist spend thousands of dollars to accommodate this desire. They pay public relations specialist to make sure their image is marketable to teenagers. Research teams are paid to be aware of new trends and new methods of reaching fans. They want to be the leaders of a new generation. Accomplishing this will satisfy the urge teens have to create distance between themselves and their parents. Teenagers want their own idols and popular artist will work to fill this role. This has been true for past and present teens. The Beetles are one of the top selling bands of all time because they filled this need. Elvis Presley is an all-time top selling artist because he became an icon for teenage girls. Madonna became the groundbreaking artist teenagers needed in the 80's. Beyoncé, Brittany Spears, Eminem, Jay-Z and Lil Wayne are more recent artist that fulfilled this need. Teenager will always look for these stars because it means so much to their identity. Parents may try to limit the influence these artist have on their children but it is difficult. No adult can monitor everything a teen does. Teenager will find a way to listen to their music. The creation of mp3 players, smartphones, and iPods makes

TEENAGE INFLUENCES

it nearly impossible to keep teenagers from their music. What adults and teens need to understand is how to handle the content of the music. Today, music lacks variety and the most popular songs are probably heard at least 5 - 10 times per day. This repetition affects anyone listening. If repetition was not an effect teaching tool then it wouldn't be used so often. School teachers, athletic coaches and many others use this method daily. So, what are the current themes being taught to teenagers through music? The short answer is spending money, sex, and partying. They glorify reckless spending and high profile lifestyles. The lifestyle of average citizens and the joys of living a normal life are rarely mentioned. It is as if a normal lifestyle isn't good enough. But this should be expected. Singers and rappers are not financial advisers. Offering information to help teens understand personal finance is the responsibility of the parents and other adults in their community. Leaving teenagers alone to learn the difference between reality and music is irresponsible. If we continue to underestimate the influence music has on teens the result will be young people suffering long term consequences. Taking musicians to court and attempting to prosecute them for our failures won't help our children. Most judges will throw out the case anyway.

The perception of school changes once children become teenagers. Most teens are starting high school by age 14 and they will experience more changes than ever before. As freshman, teens will instantly realize how young they are compared to their new peers and how much they don't know about their new environment. Completing home assignments and studying for test may not be new principles, but learning the social aspects of high school will be challenging. From their freshman year until they graduate, decisions regarding classes, sports, clubs, working, dating, and other extracurricular activities will be made. There will be more distractions than ever before and how teens manage these challenges will be important. With so much to think about, teens

41

should not have to worry about their schools ability to teach them. They should believe their school will prepare them for adulthood. Most high schools do provide their students with the resources necessary to become successful adults, but there are some that don't. High Schools across the U.S. have a greater variation in graduation rate than any other level of education. You have some states with a low 40% - 48% graduation rate and other as high as 83%. If an entire state is averaging 40% - 48% there must be schools below 40%. That is a tragedy. If all schools provide an equal opportunity to learn, then these large differences shouldn't exist. There is obviously a disconnection between the perceived value of school and everyday life. If all students felt school was necessary for future success, they would not drop out as much. High schools must be losing some level of influence and we need to make changes to increase its appeal. I believe the best way to increase influence is to offer more social studies classes. Classes that provided students with the tools to better understand social issues are very attractive. Would teens prefer a class on drugs in modern society or Latin? I believe most will prefer the first choice. I am sure after taking the class on drugs in modern society; students will be better prepared for life after school. How useful will knowing Latin be for students after graduating? High school is the one place that all teens should be able to access all the information needed to function in society. There may be many home economic classes and college prep classes available to all students, but teenagers can't learn how to manage their money in those classes. All high school curriculums should have a mandatory class on personal finance. The effect would be fewer adults in debt and less dependency of government assistance. Some students graduating from high school will not attend college and they need to be prepared for life as an adult. Teens with a good understanding of personal finance will function better in society. Until this happens, I suggest parents send their children to high schools offering the best opportunity to learn. These schools should teach how to function in society and how to succeed in college. Parents can also choose their teens electives to ensure these types of classes are included in their curriculum. Signing up teenagers for classes outside of their high school can also help. This may seem like a drastic measure but their future depends on it.

Overall, peers and friends have more influence on teenage children than anyone else. Parents have a high level of influence on their teens, but not more than friends. If parents have not established influence with their children by the time they are teens; then it will be too late to have the best impact. This doesn't mean teenagers will always follow the lead of their friends, but it does impact their decision making. Many people assume bad things will happen when teenagers influence each other, but that's not always true. Influence does not always result in direct action, but it will cause someone to battle with decision making. As children grow older, they come to realize their parents have deficiencies. Mom and Dad are no longer subject matter experts. In response to this new perception, teenagers reach out to alternative sources for information. Advances in technology have made this easier. Children are able to communicate with others using internet networking sites like Facebook, Twitter and many others. They are no longer limited to local schools and neighborhoods. In the early 1990's, teenagers had to use a desktop computer to access the World Wide Web. Today, they can use cell phones, iPads, netbooks, laptops, and many other devices. With all this access to peers inside and outside their community, teenagers will be given a variety of facts and opinions on social matters. This will cause them to challenge what they learned at home. The most popular shoes, cell phones, music, clothes and other trends are widely accepted because of peer influence. Teens don't begin dressing and speaking differently because they saw it on television. Television is just a part of the reason. Peer validation plays a big role too. What does all this have to do with personal finance? Peer influence helps to determine social norms and trends which influence the perception of money. Many effects of this influence can be found in schools. One reason some high schools are underachieving is because students have been allowed to fail. They believe education is not directly tied to financial success. If teenagers are surrounded by peers that promote educational achievement, they will be influenced to succeed in school. When they are surrounded by peers that don't believe education is the best route to financial success, the outcome will be misdirection. Now, I don't believe most children are purposely encouraging their peers to fail, but it does happen. Some children attend school because of the social environment and skip classes to socialize. Today, these students represent a greater percentage of students than previous generations. These children are hurting the schools they attend and something must be done to address this problem. A great curriculum by itself will not lead most students to success because so much more is needed. They need direction and an environment conducive to success. Few teens are able to overcome the deficiencies of their schools. The ones that do are often aided by responsible adults. Most teens lacking these resources at home will be without another tool for building a financially successful adulthood. This is how division is created between the wealthy and poor. Wealthy adults are usually surrounded by more resources leading them to financial success; while debt burden adults are not. I understand how this could seem like an exaggeration, but this is the reality of many places in the U.S. Not only do these teenagers have to overcome a lack of resources in their community; they are also receiving bad advice from their peers. This scenario can be compared to someone that has been institutionalized by prison. After being in prison for 10 plus years, most convicts return to prison. They are not prepared to function in society. This also happens to teenagers living in environments adapted to debt. They are not prepared for future financial challenges. This is the story of many debt burdened adults and growing up in this environment usually leads to bad financial decisions. The best way to battle these distractions is to provide teenagers with helpful resources. Adulthood is right around the corner.

TEENAGE INFLUENCES

5

THE FIRST CAR

I was 16 years old when we purchased my first car and it had to be the most boring car ever built. It was a standard 1987 sky blue Plymouth Reliant K car. To improve its appearance I put some illegal tents on the windows. I also added a new cd player. After getting my license and working a part time job at the movie theater, my father felt I was responsible enough to have my own car. I'm sure not having to drive me around everywhere and being able to send me out to pickup things for the house also contributed to his decision. But he had another reason for buying me a car. He thought the car would help me learn financial responsibility. I did not get this car without contributing some money towards the purchase and paying for the increase in my parent's insurance coverage. Other rules included; keeping gas in the car, meeting curfew, keeping up the maintenance and repair needs, keeping up my grades in school and never parking in the driveway. Despite all these rules, I was proud to be driving and made sure to let my friends celebrate with me. I quickly realized that owning a car was a lot of responsibility and free rides for my friends were not helpful. I needed to save money for my next car and they slowed down my progression. I couldn't wait to get rid of my old car and get a new one. I had to keep up with the ballers and show off my car on Sundays at Druid Hill Park. I had a reliable car (heck it was called a RELIANT), but it wasn't enough. This mind frame led me to making the worst purchase I could ever make. While my father was trying to teach me good personal finance lessons, I missed the most important part. Owning a car is always better than having a car payment. My father contributed to this misdirection because he would trade in his old car and get a new one every 3 years. He always ended up with a new car payment. I wasn't watching my father to find excuses for making bad financial decisions, but I did pay attention to what he was doing. I figured to get a nice car I had to get a loan from the bank, unless I became rich. My father was not the only contributing factor to my new car ambitions.

Marketers and creditors did a great job of creating a future long time customer. At 16, I bought in to their schemes. The effect of watching so many car commercials, music videos and celebrity lifestyle shows were starting to appear. I wasn't able to get a loan without a cosigner, but I had already bought into the concept. Just like I said in previous chapters; building up debt is a long process and begins before we are able to purchase anything. Growing up in Baltimore with both parents was rare amongst my peers and it still was not enough to keep me from building a future consumed by debt. Too many of us learn good financial habits after making terrible decisions. To build a better future we should consider all factors that come with getting a car.

The first question we all should ask before getting a car is; will the driver be responsible enough to handle a car? If the future owner or driver cannot follow directions from authority figures, then access to a vehicle may not be a privilege he or she is ready for. A lack of discipline will lead to expensive mistakes. Car accidents and traffic violations increase debt and money problems. We know insurance companies love when either of those events occurs because they can raise premiums and increase profits. Some accidents or traffic violations also breaks certain laws. The cost of violating these laws can be very high. Court cost, lawyer fees and bail certificates are always costly. These expenses can seriously deplete the income of any family or individual that isn't wealthy. They can go into the thousands and many people borrow money to pay for them. It doesn't matter if the money comes from a credit card, bank loan, family, friends or another creditor; it is debt. Having a car also means the driver or owner must make sure all maintenance works is performed to prevent major breakdowns. Who hasn't taken their car to a mechanic because of a major malfunction to only be told that regular maintenance could have prevented the problem? These expenses are very costly. Just getting an estimate can cost one-hundred dollars or more and that's before any repairs are made. There is also the cost of lost work hours. People with vacation hours and sick hours lose something they value. Others without some form of paid leave will not be paid for their time away from work. Public transportation expenses should also be considered. Temporarily losing a vehicle can create a need for public transportation. Once most people get a car they become dependent on their vehicles to get to work, school and anywhere else requiring travel. All these expenses can add up to more debt. The less responsible the driver is, the more these costs will add up.

The next factor that should be considered when deciding to purchase a vehicle is the cost of ownership. Car sales professionals work hard to sell vehicles and too often are portrayed as sleazy people. They don't force us to buy cars and should not be blamed when we make bad decisions. It is not their responsibility to make sure we are making an affordable purchase. They are responsible for letting us know all the defects and technical issues that may come with owning the vehicle for sale. It is our job to know our spending limit, before we arrive at the car dealership. The cost of purchasing a vehicle is not just listed on the price tag. Insurance, registration fees, fuel, maintenance, financing, repairs, and parking cost should all be considered before purchasing a vehicle. The most common cost associated with purchasing an automobile is the purchasing price. The amount of money we use to purchase vehicles should be based on long term and short term effects. Buying a vehicle without a loan will cost thousands of dollars. How does this effect savings and residual income? People should never purchase cars with all of their savings or money needed for other expenses. Cars are depreciating assets and not worth giving up financial security. Getting a car loan will create a monthly bill and limits the ability to receive compensation when selling the car. Many people use the potential monthly payment to determine if they will use a loan to purchase a vehicle. The monthly payment is important, but there are other factors to consider. The most overlook factor is the ability to handle emergencies. What happens when someone in your household experiences a drop or loss of income? What happens when an unexpected expense arises that cannot be ignored? People with savings or reserve funds for these situations are in a great position to overcome temporary hardships. What about everyone else? People that are unprepared for these situations will make late payments and the aftermath is more debt. Almost everyone makes a late car payment once and the cost is usually minimal. Being late once can cause a late fee to be charged and trigger additional interest charges. These cost increase with more frequent late payments. People that pay their car payment during the so called "grace period', the time between the due date and a late fee charge, may not realize how much extra interest accumulates. Most auto loans use a per diem interest charge during this period of time and it can add thousands of dollars to the final payoff amount. I can't tell you how many conversations I've had with customers that were surprised by these charges. They called to make one last payment and were shocked by the amount needed to pay off their loan. Those experiences were never pleasant and required all the patience and sympathy I could offer. Pier Diem was not the only charge surprising charge; late fees surprised these customers too. Late fees are not always required to be paid in addition to monthly payments, but they must be paid before the loan is completely paid off. These charges should always be considered when determining if an auto loan will be used to purchase a vehicle. Emergency expenses will always occur and not being prepared can cost thousands of dollars. In addition to the charges already mentioned, lenders have another method of increasing the cost of a loan. They use extension programs. Short term extension programs are designed to assist customers with temporary hardships by allowing payments to be skipped and added to the end of the loan. While this does help customers; it is rarely used properly. If the payments are made up before the end of the loan, then the effect will be minimal. But, if these payments are not paid as soon as possible, they will lead to more interest charges. Long term extensions are designed to help customers with long term financial struggles. These extensions grant additional years to pay off the loan. This is how a 4-5 year loan turns into a 6-8 year loan and thousands are added to the final cost of the loan. The result is paying $30,000.00 for a $20,000.00 car or even worse. I am sure there are some people that don't mind paying interest on vehicles and believe it helps to stimulate the economy, but they are a minority. Once the method of financing has been chosen, there are other costs to consider. Almost all states require vehicles to be registered and insured. Have you or any other potential driver been in an accident or received a traffic citation? How old are all the drivers and how long have they been driving? Do you have a good credit score? Is this vehicle for work and how many miles do you drive per day? Where do you live and how will your vehicle be secured and parked? Insurance companies will ask all of these questions to determine insurance premiums. If a driver is determined to be risky, the cost will be higher. Therefore, if this first car purchase is for a first time teen driver, expect high insurance payments. Adding a teenager to insurance policies will usually increase premiums between 35 and 46 percent. Once the vehicle is purchased, registered, and insured, there are other expenses to consider.

THE FIRST CAR

Today, gasoline prices are at an all time high and fuel expenses should be a part of the decision making process. Regular grade gasoline in the U.S. is around $4.00 per gallon and most new vehicles need a higher grade of gasoline to operate correctly. How often and how far will the vehicle be driven and what percent of income will be required to drive it? Car salesman are bringing more attention to this expenses compared to previous years, but the burden of understanding potential fuel cost remains with the buyer. Filling up a 15 gallon gas tank once per week will cost approximately $60.00/week or $250.00/month using regular grade gas. That is more than some car payments. Fortunately, the automotive industry is building more fuel efficient vehicles. The down side to these vehicles is the cost. They are typically more expensive than most other vehicles. Once regular oil changes, repairs, tire replacements, and other expense are accounted for; the true cost of having a vehicle is revealed. Could you imagine a car sales associate explaining all the cost of purchasing a car? No. Ignoring these expenses before purchasing a car will be very costly. Here is a story that may sound familiar. Joey recently graduated from high school and really wants a car. He will be attending a local university or college and has an internship/part time job. This job pays enough to afford at least a $250.00 monthly car payment. While in high school; Joey was a pretty good student and reasonably responsible for a teenager. Joey really wants a new car but will settle for anything less than 5-7 years old. Because Joey is a pretty good kid and has been reasonably responsible. His parents decide to purchase an $11,000.00 car with a $200.00 monthly payment. Joey will pay $50.00 per month towards the increase in their insurance policy. The loan is taken out under both parents and Joey's name to help build good credit for the future. Three months later, Joey's mother losses overtime pay and her income is reduced by 5 percent. The family can continue to assist Joey with paying insurance, but are not able to assist with any other car expenses. A few more months pass by and Joey receives a ticket for speeding and driving without his license. Joey must now pay $125.00 for the ticket and appear in traffic court for the traffic violation. After pleading to the judge for mercy, Joey only has to pay his ticket and will receive no points on his driving record. Joey's parents pay the ticket because Joey doesn't have the money, but they are starting to struggle. Their savings have been depleted because of their reduced income. One year after purchasing the car Joey is involved in an accident. Each party is equally responsible for causing the accident. The insurance company is notified and provides a rental car until Joey's car is fixed, but Joey must pay a $500.00 deductible. His insurance premiums will also be raised during the next billing period. Joey's parents can't afford to pay the entire deductible and Joey offers to pay half. As a result, Joey doesn't make the current month's loan payment. 60 days later, Joey's insurance coverage cost rises by $75.00 per month and he has to pay at least half of this increase. His parents can't afford anything more. Joey is now dependent on his car to get to work and to get to school and has no choice but to make partial payments on his auto loan to keep the car. This eventually leads to more late payments and everyone in the household has seen their credit score drop by 100 points. Joey's parents can no longer afford their monthly expenses because of cost of living increases combined with a lack of increased income. They attempt to get a loan to help ease their burdens, but are turned down because of their lower credit scores. Even if their income increases and all past due bills are paid up to date; the family's credit will take years to repair. This is how a well intentioned decision can lead to long term debt issues. Young adult in these circumstances will have debt problems before they enter the fulltime workforce. Debt accumulates overtime and car loans are often the starting point. There was another choice Joey and his parents could have made to prevent their financial problems.

Buying a car has more benefits than financing a car. Many people believe used vehicles are unattractive and unreliable. Why purchase an outdated and high maintenance vehicle? Wouldn't it be better to have a manageable monthly car payment with warranties? The answer is very simple. Overpaying for a depreciating asset never makes good financial sense. Getting out of debt begins with getting rid of old thought patterns. One of the most common misconceptions people believe in is limited time. They believe waiting for ideal circumstances will result in a lost opportunity. This way of thinking results in making a purchase based on instant gratification. To accumulate $7,500 in one year would require saving $625 per month. This may be a difficult task for an adult with debt problems, but it shouldn't be for working teenagers. In most states, teenagers are able to start working part time at the age of 15. If he or she makes $7.25 per hour for 20 hours of work per week, then $628.00 would be earned in one month. Teenagers can't be expected to save all of their income, but saving half for a year is more likely. They would be able to keep roughly $159.00 per month after putting aside money for their first car. This is a small amount of money for working adults, but a nice accumulation for teenagers. Parents could also promise to save some money for the first car purchase as an incentive or encouragement. Teenagers involved in team sports, music and any other extracurricular activities could also find ways to save for a car. There may be a need to cut down on some activities if a teen is involved in extracurricular activities for the entire year. These teens can also work part time during off seasons. Not only will a lesson in savings be learned, but this could also be an opportunity to learn about the value of money. School lessons on finance are great, but real life challenges are necessary as well. When people go to car dealerships and can guarantee the salesperson that a purchase will occur; sticker prices start to drop. Too often, consumers forget their buying power and allow the seller to control sales. They allow their desires and emotions to take over. Money being offered today will always be better than money promised in the future. All car salesmen believe this. Their income is based on completing a sale. These salesmen don't want to take the chance of losing the sale by delaying the process another day. Understanding this can be the difference between leaving with a car priced at $10,000 but only paying $7,500 or leaving with a $7,500 car. Getting a great deal for the vehicle is not the only benefit to buying without a loan. Complete ownership instantly gives the owner an asset and increases their net worth. Until auto loans are paid off the vehicle belongs to the bank and usually cannot be considered an asset. What better gift could be given to a teenager but to give them an asset before they are adults? Sure it may not be as great as thousands of dollars in savings, but it will always be better than increasing their debt. The same is true for adults purchasing a car for the first time. Whether you are buying a first car for a teenager or yourself, owning a car is better than getting a loan. Take a moment to evaluate your assets versus debts. Those with car loans will usually have more debts than assets. Car ownership also creates a fallback option to guarantee a loan. If all other options for getting out of a difficult financial crisis are not available, then a loan against your car comes in handy. I would never recommend someone to take out a loan to pay off debts, but I do understand there are situations where it makes sense. Having resources to combat difficult financial situations is a sure way to increase your financial freedom and stay away from debt problems. Assets are always better than liabilities and it is imperative to consider all factors when purchasing a first car.

THE FIRST CAR

6

AFTER HIGH SCHOOL

Graduating from high school is a good accomplishment and marks a very important transition from childhood to adulthood. Many parents may not view their 18 year old teenager as an adult, but financial institutions and other businesses do. Anyone over the age of 18 can get a loan, credit card, rent an apartment or make any other decisions that will affect their financial status. They don't need parental approval. While most of these financial decisions may be avoided for a few more years, several will require immediate attention.

College, trade schools, and military careers are all life changing options affecting the financial stability of young adults. For years they have heard sales pitches related to post high school graduation life. The amount of advertisements and words of advice young adults receive about post high school graduate choices are countless. These influences will have a large effect on which route is chosen and how much debt they will have to overcome. College, trade schools and military careers all come with a cost. Ignoring them could lead to serious debt issues. So how much does each option really cost?

The majority of young adults graduating from high school will attend college because it's their best chance to acquiring a good paying job. Most jobs paying over $50,000 per year require some level of college education and sometimes that's not enough. Using college to get good paying jobs is a widely accepted practice in the United States. Parents and children understand the importance of obtaining a college education in our society, but they are not the only people who understand its importance. Investors and business executives at colleges understand how much society values post high school education. Their job is to make sure these schools maximize their earning potential at our expense. Most colleges and universities are for profit organizations and the cost to attend these institutions are at an all time high. The issue all people planning on attending these institutions must address is the cost of an education versus the reward. Is getting a particular degree from a specific college worth the cost? The answer to this question depends on personal values, finances and other demographics. I will only be addressing the last two because the only values I can defend are my own. I will never question anyone about their desire to obtain a college degree. Once we remove spiritual and social values, is the cost of college really worth it? Is getting a college degree worth spending $50,000 to $70,000? What if most jobs available only pays $30,000 per year? There are many unknown factors that must be considered before answering the question. What is the potential for earnings to increase? What are the cost of living expenses where the person will reside? How are college expenses being paid? All these questions and more should be answered before a person chooses what school they will attend. If the effect of paying for school results in a long term financial loss, then a bad financial decision was made. According to College Board, the 2010-2011 average total costs (including tuition, fees, room and board) were $16,140 for students attending four-year public colleges and universities in-state and $28,130 out-of state. Four-year private colleges and universities were estimated at $36,993. The estimate for other fees and books was approximately $4,000. In four years a college student can potentially amassed approximately $64,500 - $148,000 of debt before they earn their first paycheck. Even if we assume 50 percent of these cost are covered with scholarships, $32,250 - $74,000 of these expenses still need to be paid. Parents and students with the ability to save funds for school ahead of time will be in the best position to handle these costs, but they are a minority. What about the average American family that don't have the funds to pay for school expenses? What are the long term effects on these students? The short answer is long term debt. During the debt building years, which is between the age of 18 and 32, people are expected to increase their debt as they build a new lifestyle. The best way to minimize long term debt problems created during this time span is to avoid as much debt as possible.

So how does a person without a large savings minimize debt growth when trying to obtain a college degree? The best way is to graduate from high school with a 3.8 or better GPA. There are millions of scholarships for students with the best grades and there is no better way to deal with these costs. Great grades usually lead to less debt and easier paths to financial freedom. Sure there is no guarantee that having a 4.0 GPA will lead to all college expenses being covered, but it does increase the odds. Once the idea of graduating with a little debt as possible is accepted, then it will be easier to understand why getting great grades is so important. If there is one concept all teens understand it's the idea of keeping more of the money they earn. A doctor making $125,000 per year while having $100,000 in school debt to payoff is not financially comfortable. The same doctor would be much happier having to pay off $30,000 of school debt. What person wouldn't want to keep $95,000 of their income compared to $25,000? If that's not motivation for getting great grades I don't know what is.

Teenagers also must be taught about the long lasting effects of building too much debt before 25. Why? What is the first thing most people do when they graduate from college? They buy a home, car and build their own family? Graduating from college usually coincides with a major lifestyle change and this is when most long term debt is built. Paying off school loans while building this adult lifestyle is very expensive and often times leads to years of debt problems. We have heard the stories about doctors and lawyers having to file bankruptcy. The inability of graduate students and people with PhD's to find work is a regular news headline. Attaining a post graduate degree no longer guarantees the ability to pay off school loans. There are other choices available for students wanting to pursue a college degree and more. Instead of going into serious debt to pursue a degree, high school graduates can begin their journey towards riches at a community college. There are very few differences between a four year college and a two year college during freshman and sophomore years. The biggest difference is the cost, but the curriculums are very similar. Based on College Board, the average cost of tuition for two year colleges is $2,544 per semester. That is approximately $13,600 less than the lowest average for four year schools. Attending community college before transferring to a four year college could result in avoiding $27,000 of debt. Some people perceive community colleges as an extension of high school, but for the most part this is a false perception. They key to finding which school best aligns with post graduate goals is to research the offered curriculum and successful transfer rate. This information is not hard to find and is usual available on the schools website or through a brochure. Many universities and colleges will even recommend particular community colleges they preferred to accept transfer students from. People should always explore all options when considering going to college because it could be save thousands of dollars.

Trade schools and tech institutions are popular alternatives to college for high school graduates. They are attractive to young adults looking to enter the workforce quickly. Instead of spending four or more years learning to attain a bachelor degree; these schools offer the chance to begin working after one or two years. Some people attend trade school because they need to find a job before going to a four year school. Others understand college isn't for them and not worth the cost. No matter reason people chose to attend these schools, everyone should attempt to make a good financial decision. Many trade schools are less expensive than colleges, but are not the best option for some young adults. How much does attending a trade school usually cost? Trade school fees vary based on several factors such as programs, location, withdrawal fees, reputation, etc. Some are more expensive than two year colleges and some are less. The most important factor in estimating the value of investing in trade schools is the result of completing their offered programs. Does the school have a working relationship with hiring employers and reputable businesses? How often do graduates find jobs after graduating? What are their salaries? All of these and more questions need to be answered when deciding which trade school to attend. Trade schools offering courses that will fulfill the needs of the current economy are the best. Becoming a real estate agent through these programs would have been a great idea in the late 90's and early 2000's, but today the rewards are not worth the risk for most people. Computer technicians, programmers, radiation therapists, diagnostic medical sonographers and auto mechanics (hybrid and electric specialist) are all highly sought professions averaging over $45,000 per year. The best trade schools offer certificate programs for these occupations. Paying $5,000 - $10,000 for completing a trade school program and getting a job that pays $45,000 per year is a good investment. In this scenario, all school debt could be paid off within a year and money could be saved to pursue a college degree. Taking this route could lead to financial freedom, but there is another variable that may cause this scenario to fail. It is very difficult for people to stop going to conventional schools and return to the same type of learning environment. Many people find themselves talking about going back to school after long breaks. Most will never go back or finish. There are several reasons this happens. Going back to school is a lifestyle change many people are not prepared to take on. They begin their journey back to school with so much enthusiasm but fail to maintain it. This mentality must be overcome to prevent a financial loss. The goal is to have a net increase from education investments. When curriculums are not completed, there is a net loss. When students pay to attend trade schools but don't qualify for jobs that will cover school expenses; there is a net loss. After making the mistake of overpaying for a certification program, many people go further into debt by pursuing a college degree. People in these situations often think they will go to college and overcome their current debt problems. Unfortunately, the opposite occurs. School debt continues to increase while six figure salary jobs are nowhere to be found. There are two reasons these jobs are so difficult to acquire for new college graduates. They require work experience and good credit standings. In today's job market, employers can use credit reports to screen all applicants. Too much debt and frequent delinquencies can lead to loss opportunities. Ironic isn't it; pursuing a degree to become a better job candidate resulting in losing job opportunities. Choosing to attend trade school instead of the other options can be a great choice, if it doesn't result in more debt than income. The goal should always be to make a choice which allows the best chance at financial freedom.

Are the phrases, "Be all that you can be" and "The Few the proud", familiar to you? Military commercials have been flooding the airwaves for years. They've created a popular alternative to school for many young adults. The most common selling points are the ability to pay for college and travel around the world. What young adult doesn't want to travel and go to school? Being able to leave home and earn a decent income is attractive to any young adult. People also seek to join the military to defend and honor our country. These people feel obligated to protect our freedoms and we should be thankful for their service. But, what impact will this decision have on their financial stability? For starters, all branches of the military enforce laws to prevent financial problems. They believe financial problems can affect military readiness. The military has setup regulations to make sure active soldiers are financially responsible. Soldiers found in bad financial standings can be discharged or receive other forms of discipline. Regulations alone cannot guarantee financial freedom, but they do encourage financial responsibility. It is not a coincidence that most of people in the military have good credit scores and receive more loans than civilians. Honor is a principle most people in the military hold high and honoring promises is a duty. Other financial benefits of enlisting are the grants offered to pay for college. We've already discussed how expensive it is to attend college and the military alleviates this matter all together. With so many opportunities to build financial stability, what are the possible negative impacts of joining the military?

The lifestyle of our soldiers is very expensive and filled with frequent opportunities to increase credit debt. The cost associated with frequent travel and communication is much higher for military families than it is for civilians. Switching schools and daycare providers creates expenses that are difficult to overcome. Not all daycare centers provide services for the same cost and frequent travel can increase this expense. Many daycare providers require an upfront deposit and large down payments to accept new children. Changing schools can also be expensive because of different curriculum requirements and extracurricular activity expenses. Military families also have a greater need for communication devices. Cell phone bills and online video chatting services are usually more costly for military families. The constant travel required for active duty troops create a greater need for these devices. Most cell phone providers do provide additional discounts for members of the military, but they do not totally offset the cost. Another expense to consider when evaluating the cost of joining the military is travel expenses. People in the military are often separated from their family due to relocation requirements. This creates the need to use airlines and train stations more often than the average person in the U.S. The cost of flying is higher than it has ever been, but not visiting family members is not an option for many troops. While cost of living expenses for military workers is increasing, their rate of pay has only increased by 1.4%, according to military.com. This leads many troops to seek loans. More than 25 percent of military personnel have $10,000 in credit card debt. Another 10 percent have more than $20,000. Approximately one-third of the military will admit to experiencing debt problems. Many service members are desperate enough to get payday or auto title loans. A Defense Department study has revealed; members of the military use payday loans three times as often as civilians. Having such a high level of access to credit requires discipline and too often our soldiers use credit to solve financial problem. When most civilians experiences debt problems their options are limited, but military workers are given more options. In many cases, they are forced to find ways to eliminate debt and this just leads to more long term debt. The long term effects are persistent debt problem. But, it is possible to use the military to create financial freedom. All that is required is discipline.

   In addition to trade school, college and the military; high school graduates have another option to choose. Some young adults prefer to skip all the previously mentioned options to enter the workforce full-time. Entering the workforce with a high school degree has been spoken against for decades. The options are very limited for people without a college degree or professional certification. The positions available for high school graduates usually offer low pay and little room for growth. So, how does entering the workforce with only a high school diploma effect long term financial stability? Most of you reading this are probably thinking this route guarantees a lifestyle filed with debt, but that is not always the case. Entering the workforce with only a high school diploma has several effects on financial stability. According to Payscale.com, people with only a high school diploma averaged an entry level pay of

$33,485 in 2009. The type of lifestyle this level of pay can support depends on several factors such as location, family structure, total household income and employment type. A family may be able to exceed a paycheck to paycheck lifestyle in Ohio but not in New York City. At a pay rate of $33,485 per year most cities in the U.S. are affordable living options for single family households. However, this level of pay would not be enough to cover basic living expenses for any other household type. If the average starting pay for high school graduates is the only source of income for a multiple person households; the effect will often be a partial dependency on debt and government assistance. This is a terrible starting point for any young adult and can lead to a life filled with debt problems. Single household high school graduates are not off the hook either. They may also have a difficult time with debt. The best way for these individuals to avoid future debt problems is to go back to school or completing some professional training courses. This will increase their eligibility for higher paying positions. One reason so many high school graduates fall off this path is complacency and envy. There is a lot of pressure for 18 and 19 year old adults to match the lifestyles of their new older peers. They no longer spend significant time with other teenager because eight plus hours of the day are spent with working adults. This new environment will often lead to desires for a more expensive lifestyle. Like most people, they want to fit in with their new peers. Saving for school is no longer a high priority for many people in this situation and the majority of their income becomes is used to pay bills. Once their finances heads in this direction, it will become difficult to reverse. They will be on a path to a lifestyle filled with debt. A lack of pay increases will create another challenge. According to Payscale.com, the average pay increase without additional certifications or educational achievements is $1,755 or 1.3 percent per year. That is less than the rate of inflation or cost of living increases for almost all U.S. cities. Keeping up with the lifestyle of already established adults is expensive and the lack of pay increases will make it difficult for young adults to avoid debt problems. The best choice for many of these young adults is to remain living with their providers, if allowed to.

7

MOVE OUT OR STAY HOME

I moved out of my parents' house when I was 18. This was immediately after my freshman year in college and it was a terrible financial decision. Working was never a problem for me because I've consistently held on to jobs since I was 14 years old. I felt I was too mature to be home and needed to move into my own home. So, I talked to my friend Roland and we agreed to share an apartment for a year or two. It only took 1 year for me to fall into financial trouble because of my decision to move out. I was paying for my education, apartment, car repairs, food, cable, cell phones, insurance and many other bills with limited income. I was in such a rush to get out of my parents' house that I did not consider the true cost of independence. I suffered the consequences of my actions. I defaulted on my first credit card, my grades were only average and my social life was almost nonexistent. I did learn some good lesson from this experience, but I could have avoided so many problems by just staying home another year. My parents were not pushing me to move out or asking me to pay household bills. I really didn't have to move out. My dad told me I didn't have to rush out, but I was not going to change my mind. My story is similar to many others stories and it's often the beginning of long term debt problems. Moving out or staying home are decisions many young adults have to make. The consequences can be long lasting and all factors should be considered before making such an important decision. So, what kind of factors should be considered?

All young adults need to evaluate if they can afford to move into their own home. There are many expenses outside of rent, utilities, food, transportation and communication that must be accounted for while determining the affordability of leaving home. Young adults often don't realize how expensive independence can be. They will usually borrow money to compensate for their unpreparedness. After all the previously mentioned expenses are paid, is there money left for dating, eating out, shopping, grooming, transportation repairs, medical and dental checkups, cable, internet, traveling and entertainment? It is unrealistic to believe a young adult is not going to date or go to parties on a long term basis. Young adults don't realize how much they are provided for while living with their providers. Moving out without this knowledge will lead to debt problems and more bills for their parents. The first people most young adults will reach out to for help are parents. As young adults, they are more costly than when they lived home. Most parents prefer their teens to stay home to prevent these types of scenarios. This is why it is important to discuss the true cost of moving with all young adults looking to leave home.

Once all expenses are accounted for, it is time to consider how they will be paid for. If there is no source of income to cover these expenses, then the decision is easy. The young adult should stay home. How can anyone plan to cover the expenses of moving out without having a source of income? For everyone else with a source of income, the answers to these next questions are essential to this evaluation process. Will I make enough money to pay for my new expenses? How many work hours are needed to pay all bills? Will I stay with this company if it does not fulfill my career goals? If I am laid off will I receive unemployment? The first question can be answered with either yes or no because there is no other option. Either enough money can be earned to cover expenses or it can't. If the answer is no, there is no reason to move on to the next questions. However, if the answer is yes, there must be consideration for the time needed to earn this money. They must realize all the limitations of working students. Working students should not sacrifice their learning potential because of the need to cover lifestyle expenses. If obtaining a degree or certification is the top priority, then work should not cause deviation. It is possible to work and attend school simultaneously, but work should not negatively affect school performance. The amount of hours a person can work without experiencing a mental and physical breakdown varies for each individual. Some people can handle 60 hour work weeks and some can barley handle 40. Working too many hours will usually lead to quitting or being fired. Any young adult person providing for themselves can't afford either to happen. Another contributor to quitting or being fired is career satisfaction. Many people begin experiencing financial problems after changing jobs or quitting because of dissatisfaction. People that have been self dependent for years usually have a good understanding of local job markets. Others are too inexperienced to understand. Young adults often believe they will find another job as easily as they found their current job. This perception leads many young adults to leave their jobs when dissatisfied. The consequences can be very costly and leads to serious financial problems. Understanding the importance of keeping a job is crucial. Job dissatisfaction should not be a reason for making a terrible financial decision. Young adults should also have a plan for losing employment. Landlords do not care about the reason for the inability to pay rent or mortgage. They expect to get paid when there payment is due and losing work is not their problem. Layoffs are a natural part of our economy and having a job with unemployment benefits is essential. Young adults usual don't have enough money in savings to compensate for being laid off. They need their employers to pay into unemployment benefit programs.

Short term disability and paid sick time off are other benefits young adults should demand. Many young adults are evicted because they lacked these benefits. Once affordability is addressed, the next factor needing evaluation is timing.

There is no standard for when people should move into their own home, but certain circumstances can lead to good and bad timing. Bad timing is moving out while there is still an opportunity to stay home and save money. Racing towards independence can lead to these missed opportunities. If parents are willing to help their young adult children save money; then why not stay a little longer. There is a point when people should seek out their independence, but I am not in favor of rushing the process. As long as people are able to tolerate another adult living in their home, the only reason to leave is the need for independence. Many people may call me crazy, but I think it is good for a young adult to live with someone assisting with the moving out process. Many parents would be willing to allow their adult children to live under their care longer if there is a reasonable exit strategy. What parent wouldn't want to setup their children for the best chance to succeed on their own? I am opposed to young adults living in a household contributing to irresponsibility. Enabling young adults to develop irresponsible behaviors is a disservice to society. While it is possible for people living in this environment to become responsible adults; the opposite is more likely. Young adults leaving home ill equipped to deal with real world challenges is another example of bad timing. This example is the worst of the two. Some young adults miss an opportunity to save by leaving home, but leaving unprepared usually produces long term financial problems. Where do we think most of these young adults will go after they are not able to take care of themselves? The less prideful individuals will attempt to return back to the home where they were being provided for. The others will likely fall victim to people seeking to take advantage of their weakness. Some people are only happy when other people depend on them; these relationships can create a feeling of supremacy and relevance. This is one of the many reasons some people develop relationships similar to a prostitute and pimp. The prostitute feels secure under the care of the pimp and makes sure to follow his or her lead. We all depend on each other for survival, but unprepared young adults are more dependent than others. Creditors also have ways to exploit those struggling with financial responsibility. One of the first places many adults experiencing financial problems go to for help are banks or loan companies. Too often loans are perceived as the best method to solve temporary money problems. The problem with this philosophy is the true issue has not been addressed and debt problems will linger. Obtaining debt to provide relief from a financial burden is never a good remedy for people lacking good financial discipline. Many people borrow hundreds or thousands of dollars for relief and are never learn how to avoid loan dependency. Banks love this habit. They will earn 2 or 3 times the value of their loans because of it. Learning the skills needed to avoid these debt traps before moving out is essential to financial well-being. This behavior is a characteristic of good timing. Good timing is a combination of financial readiness, social readiness and maximized saving potential. I learned about the impact of good timing while working at the bank. Several wealthy customers would share their stories of financial success with me. One gentleman's story stuck with me for a long time. He began his story with a decision he made during his senior year in college. He decided to continue living with his parents after graduating. He promised he would leave after 18 months, if he found a job immediately after finishing school. Fortunately, he found a job a few weeks before his graduation. His new job paid him $30,000 per year and he didn't have to pay many bills. His parents only required him to pay his car insurance and cable bill. During this 18 month tenure he was able to save $17,000. That may seem unrealistic, but only requires saving $944 of the

$1875 he brought home monthly. I assumed he didn't have much of a social life, but I was wrong. He had enough money to date and live like any other twenty year old. It didn't take much time to find an apartment because he was constantly searching. He used $9,000 to pay one year's rent and used the remaining $8,000 to purchase a used car. With his rent and car paid covered, his monthly expenses were limited to utilities, food, clothes, cable service, auto insurance and cell phone coverage. His monthly expenses totaled $600 per month once he accounted for gas. He was left with $1,275 per month. Saving became a habit and enabled him to accumulate wealth. He eventually went on to buy a house, get married and raise children. But he never earned more than $50,000 per year. Today, he is a millionaire. He credited all his success to one decision. This wasn't an easy choice, but he ignored his desire for immediate independence. He chose to stay home for 18 months. His story has stuck with me for years. He became a millionaire in 23 year, yet never earned a six figure salary. Some of you are probably thinking his wife earned a huge salary, but she never made more than $50,000 per year. However; she did help by buying into her husband's saving philosophy. His parents helped too. They were willing to assist him and put off their own desires. By allowing him to stay home for 18 months, they enabled him to ease into self-reliance. Some parents believe once their adult children have the ability to care for themselves, it is time for them to leave. While there is nothing wrong with that belief; I hope the financial well-being of the child is considered. Every parent has the right to decide when to take back their extra bedroom. There is no standard timeframe to follow, but all parents should be careful when making this decision. Staying too long can create tension and leaving too early can create a missed opportunity. The best way for young adults and providers to determine the correct time to part ways is to talk about it. Having several conversations allows all everyone to voice their wants and needs. This dialog will help to avoid unnecessary conflict that will lead to a bad decision. Another factor contributing to this story was patience. The urge to leave home and the rules of another adult is very powerful and influential. It was crucial for him to determine how much longer he could follow the rules of another adult. By understanding this, he maximized his savings potential. Six months would have been too soon and two years would have aggravated his family. Every person in this situation must determine what their maximum saving potential is, but it requires an honest assessment. This level of self evaluation may not be possible for teens, but should be possible for all young adults.

This process should also include an assessment of social readiness. Once all financial aspects of moving out have been addressed, there is still a need to evaluate the mental ability to handle independence. Life as an independent adult is a drastic lifestyle change. This is a new environment. There are no barriers to hide the ugliest parts of society. Self-confidence and personal values are constantly targeted. People attempt to control each other. Some start small and large wars to oppose the opinions of others. Sympathy for tough breaks like job loss is minimal outside of family and friends. Landlords and bill collectors want what's owed to them and will pursue debt until it is paid. Sad stories and unfortunate circumstances are not their problem. Dreams are often unrealized and most people don't end up rich and famous. Adulthood is far removed from the lifestyles of movie characters. Reality is much more complex. There is also a beautiful side of adulthood. If life was all negative, why would people pursue the beautiful aspects of life? Some people are able to live their dreams and agree with the values of others. Not everyone experiences major financial, physical and emotional problems. The key to being mentally prepared for an independent adult lifestyle is to recognize both the favorable and unfavorable aspects of life. Bad things will happen to good people and good thing will happen to bad people.

Understanding multiple aspects of adult life contributes to good personal finance habits. There are many schemes designed to persuade people to leave a path of financial freedom; so it is important to recognize methods of persuasion. Marketers are required to study psychology and philosophy so they can create methods to influence consumption. To overcome their tactics we must also understand the influential factors of adult consumption.

8

ADULT INFLUENCES

Childhood dreams are expected to be realized once we become adults. Those dreams are often the standard which we use to measure personal success. We often begin this evaluation by questioning our social relevance. Have you ever found yourself comparing your professional success to your peers? If so, you are judging your social relevance. It is normal for this to occur, so don't feel bad. Few adults have the ability to disregard social status and many of these people are mentally unstable or monks. To have a total disregard towards society, a person would not live according to laws, social norms or much else outside of survival needs. Government and social structure has little significance to these people. Therefore, we must include social relevance when examining the spending habits of most adults. If this wasn't true, there would be no need for different houses, clothes, family structures, toys and anything else that is produced. We would be pleased with living a lifestyle identical to our neighbors.

Some people may consider themselves to be anti-government, anti-establishment, rebels or anything similar, but they still care about social relevance. Those Yankee hats, Champaign bottles, Prada shoes, Gucci bags, Huntsman suits, Under Armor sweatshirts, Lexus, Mercedes, Fords, Hondas, Jeeps, Prius, single family homes and condos were purchased with thoughts of public perception. Our possessions are used as a measure of social and financial achievement. We have been taught to believe luxurious possessions equate to success and wealth. This belief drives us to obtain possessions that will increase our debt. We don't pursue debt because of a desire to be poor. The motivator is the appearance of success. We like surrounding ourselves with successful people and expensive possessions. Most wealthy people trust others that are wealthy and everyone desires to be a part of their inner circle. People wearing outdated clothes and living in small houses are often viewed as poor. They are rejected by society or judged to be lazy and worthless. This perception is formed before any conversation occurs. The opposite is also true. Millionaires don't usually hang out with poor people and the poor usually don't befriend millionaires. Some people create personas based on a false reality to change this social norm. They wear the newest cloths and purchase expensive homes to present an illusion of wealth. This illusion creates opportunities to build relationships with wealthy people. It also helps to build business partnerships. To see this habit we only need to turn on the television.

Many reality television celebrities are not wealthy before they appear on television, but are pressured to appear wealthy. This pressure influences them to lead a luxurious lifestyle before they amass any wealth. They often end up filling bankruptcy due to their short lived success and luxurious lifestyle. The same holds true for many musicians, actors, sports entertainers and others made popular through media.

The federal government also borrows and spends money to appear more financially stable than it truly is. If you need some convincing, look no further than the federal budget deficit. This habit has also shown up overseas. Greece had to be bailed out by international banks because of this behavior. We can also observe this behavior in our local communities. If we look around with an honest perception, we will find people attempting to appear wealthy. It may be a neighbor, friend, family member, co-worker, boss, or even us. On the contrary; some chose to run away from this perception by purchasing things that are far from luxurious.

ADULT INFLUENCES

We have all heard stories about millionaires driving old cars and wearing clothes from thrift stores. These individuals purposely create an image to mask their wealthy, but their actions are also influenced by society. They are using a social norm to create a false perception. Whether we are attempting to create an image of wealth or poverty; those actions are ultimately influenced by society. The attention that comes with a wealthy lifestyle also influences people to live above their means. It's not all about rubbing shoulders with rich folk. Most people enjoy the idea of fame. They want to be adored and followed by millions on Twitter. Thoughts of being on talk shows and attending the most exclusive parties fill their minds. These ambitions can be very costly. How much social relevance is able to influence us often depends heavily on our religious beliefs.

Religion is another important and influential part of adult decision making. All children may not have a choice in which religion they will follow, but adults can serve the deity of their preference. With over 260,000 registered religious groups in the world, this choice can sometimes be complicated. The reason for choosing to be a part of a religion can be based on family, friends or personal comfort. People may work endlessly to change our beliefs, but the final decision is always personal. Despite this choice, all religions have one thing in common. They all have a philosophy with lifestyle guidelines. Financial discipline, monetary offerings and serving are a few common themes of these groups. All people may not follow these guidelines to the same degree, but their religious beliefs will affect all decisions. Religious people are required to consider their beliefs before making any decisions and there is no exception for finances. Will buying this car take away from my family or prevent me from giving my weekly offering or tithe? Am I giving enough to support my local congregation? These are questions many religious people ask themselves while making important financial decisions. The effect religious beliefs will have on personal finances varies based on the religion being followed. I would have to write another book to analyze the financial practices of all religions, so I will only deal with the most popular groups. The most popular religions as of 2010 are Christianity, Islam, Hinduism, Buddhism, Sikhism and Judaism.

Christians are people that believe in one GOD and follow the teachings of Jesus Christ. There are many different man made denominations of Christianity, but they can usually fall under four categories; Catholic, Orthodox, Protestant, and Other. All of them may have slight differences in regards to their collections (offering) practices, but they all teach Christians to give a portion of their assets to the church. Many refer to this practice as giving alms; which is also referred to as offering or tithe. The church is then to use the offerings to support congregational needs, missions and poor citizens. Many Christians do not believe in a required specific percentage of assets to be offered. But all offerings are to come from the heart. "So let each one give as he purposes in his heart, not grudgingly or of necessity; for God loves a cheerful giver" (2 Corinthians chapter 6 verse 7 NKJV). Christians also believe they shouldn't place riches or wealth above GOD. "But they that will be rich fall into temptation and a snare, and into many foolish and hurtful lusts, which drown men in destruction and perdition. For the love of money is the root of all evil: which while some coveted after, they have erred from the faith, and pierced themselves through with many sorrows" (1 Timothy chapter 6 verses 9&10 NKJV). After reading these scriptures someone might think all Christians are good money managers, but that depends on how faithful a person is to their beliefs. There can also be situations where people give too much and neglect their other responsibilities. Based on the Bible, that action is considered disobedient or unfaithful. Christians shouldn't have a lot of debt or allow money to take away from their Christian duties. "Let no debt remain outstanding, except the continuing debt to love one another, for he who loves his fellowman has fulfilled the law" (Romans chapter 13 verse 8 NIV). Overall, Christianity requires followers to be good money managers. Lacking good financial habits can lead to a separation from GOD.

Muslims, which is the name for people that follow Islam, believe in one GOD (Allah). Their book of doctrine is the Holy Qur'an and it is believed to be the word of Allah through the prophet Muhammad. I am not a Muslim and will not provide any quotes directly from the Qur'an to avoid offending any Muslim readers. I have had the opportunity to read some of the Qur'an with my Muslim friends and those are the resources of my findings. Now back to Muslim practices. Muslims follow the practice of zakat, which is a giving practice. This practice instructs Muslims to give a certain percentage of their business, savings earnings and assets to the poor. Muslims also practice sadakat, which is an offering to support the spreading of Islam. Muslims, like Christians, have a high regard for intent. Both believe a givers attitude towards giving is essential to their practices. Muslims are also encouraged to abstain from gambling to prevent forsaking their other duties. With all the instruction regarding giving and money management; a faithful Muslim would be expected to live a financially responsible lifestyle. How closely these principles are followed depends on the faith of each Muslim.

Hinduism is a complex belief system predominately found in India. For the most part, Hindus believe in one GOD while accepting the presence of others. While there are no specific universal guidelines to define Hinduism, there is a belief in karma. Karma is generally believed to be the process of cause and effect. Hindus believe if you do good deeds the result will also be good effects and this holds true for finances. Because there are no standards set for giving, all followers are instructed to give from the heart. They believe good will come from their charity. Having the ability to be charitable to others requires some level of financial discipline.

Buddhism is another religion with a wide variety of practices, but most are based on the teachings of Buddha (Siddhartha Gautama). The ultimate goal is to escape the cycle of suffering and rebirth through enlightenment. The two major groups of Buddhism are Theravada ("The School of the Elders") and Mahayana ("The Great Vehicle"). Buddhist believe in karma, but there are differences in practices and specific understanding of karma. Buddhist do not believe in indulging in the riches and wealth of this world. Many followers live very meager lifestyles. The most popular example is the monk lifestyle. Monks are some of the most disciplined people in the world. They practice asceticism, abstinence from worldly pleasures. All levels of Buddhism require followers to practice financial responsibility.

Judaism is a one GOD based religion practiced by Jewish people. They follow the teachings of GOD through Moses; which is also a part of Christian and Islamic history. There is some division within Judaism concerning what defines a Jew. Some people believe a person has to be born of a Jewish (race) mother to be considered a Jew; while others believe a person can become a Jew through conversion. Judaism does have certain financial principles accept by all followers. In Judaism, money is just another tool used in positive or negative manners. They believe wealthy followers are responsible for helping the poor and should not lend to other Jews for gain (usury). Jewish laws regarding lending to non- Jews differ based on belief. Some people believe it is ok to lend with interest while others do not. Offering and tithing was a practice followed by ancient Jews, but most modern followers do not believe they are obligated to give a set percentage of their assets. Based on these guidelines most Jews are expected to be financially responsible. All these religions have an effect on the financial practice of their followers, family and traditions can also influence their financial habits.

Family and traditions are an influential part of financial decision making for most adults. Our family members are usually the first people we learn our financial habits from. As we have discussed in previous chapters, family habits influence young children and teens. Once we leave the protection of our parents; those habits we learned will show up when we make purchases. The way we celebrate holidays, chose schools, purchase cars, buy homes and other spending trends are influenced by our families. Some of us wouldn't know Black Friday exists without family members. Last minute shopping is often a habit learned from parents. Family spending habits even impact our lifestyle choices. Wealthy families usually produce wealthy adults and poor families usually produce non wealthy adults. The primary contributor to each outcome is not financial status, it is their financial habits. Some adults raised in wealthy households have become poor once they left the protection of their parents. Some adults that were raised in poor households have been able to become wealthy. However; those outcomes are usually an exception instead of the norm. Breaking away from these learned habits are very difficult. We were taught these habits for 20 plus years. The only way to break away from this cycle is to be exposed to and adapt new financial habits. Our buying habits are not the only part of our financial decision making affected by our family. We also have to deal with the financial matters of family members. Who takes on the expense of caring for elderly people in our families? Who picks up the funeral cost when a relative dies and leaves no money? Who often is the beneficiary when someone dies and leaves an inheritance? Families are structured in many different ways but all have some level of codependency. Some families depend heavily on all adults taking care of themselves; while others depend on all adults working together. Many families need teenagers to assist with household expenses, but others do not. There are four classifications all families fall under which describe their financial structure; intra-household, multi-household, generational and total inclusion. When a family shares financial gains and losses exclusively with members of their household, they fall under the intra-household financial classification. These families do not consider people outside of their household in their financial decision making. This does not mean outside family members will not receive gifts; there just is no regard for their financial status. People that move away from their hometown and family can find themselves following this model. People that share financial gains and losses with some members of their family but not all, fall under the multi-household classifications. This is probably the most popular family financial structure in the United States. These families plan their finances while considering a select number of family members. They help some family members pay for college, funerals, weddings and other large expenses; while ignoring other relatives. Disputes and isolation within a family can lead to excluding certain family members from being included in financial planning. Inheritance is a common practice used within families that fall under the generational classification. These families only share financial gains and losses based on generation; which is usually determined by the average age between a mother and her child. There is no standard to determine how all people define family generation. But, most nations follow some type of guideline. No matter which measure is used, these people only share financial gains and losses with family members of the next generation. They do not give loans and share wealth with their peers, but do with younger family members. An adult in this family could save money to ensure all their nieces or nephews are able to pay for college, but would not save money to assist their siblings. The elder members of these families often list their children and grandchildren as heirs of estates instead of siblings. There is always a passing down of assets and debts instead of any lateral movement. Total Inclusion is a practice commonly found within royal families. This occurs when families share financial gains and losses with all family members. Bloodline is the usual method of determining membership. These families are usually invested in the growth and survival of a bloodline. They work together through estates and business to ensure their family thrives as long as possible. When financial decisions are made in this family, the wellbeing of all members is considered. All these structures effect the financial decisions we make. Understanding the impact our families have on us will help us with all financial planning.

Most adult workers I've encountered obtained jobs as a means to an end. They are not working in a field or position based on career fulfillment and come to work solely for monetary purposes. While some people develop a liking towards their occupation; many will admit the preference for another. Our society is built on the pursuit of wealth and requires people to work solely based on this goal. How would our country operate if all citizens could choose their job? How many lower income jobs openings would be filled? Most of these jobs would be vacant because most of us car more about salaries. Whether we are passionate about our jobs or not; we all make decisions based on similar concerns. Job security is a major concern for all workers. When most of us believe our jobs are stable we tend to have a more careless attitude towards spending. We are confident our next paycheck is only a few days away and do not frequently plan for unknown scenarios. Some of us may fear losing our jobs, but we still believe finding another will be relatively easy. Many of our financial decisions are based on this confidence. Today, we may talk about the return of the Great Depression or economic collapse, but our actions don't show our faith in those events occurring. Our faith in long term stability runs deep our minds despite a failing economy and all-time highs in job layoff statistics. If we thought otherwise it would reflect in our assets and less of us would be in a state of financial ruin. Our spending habits would reflect a high level of focus on securing necessities and disregarding wants. We would prepare ourselves for the possibility of job loss and make sure our debt levels were low to prevent losses. Overall we have a lot of faith in the United States economic system despite small protest and political debates. In fact, some of these protests are in place with a goal of increased wealth for all U.S. citizens and not stabilizing the economy. They worry about of the morality of business policies more than the survival of our economy. Some people cloak their confidence in our economy by claiming to be content with being poor. They claim to be content with their financial struggles because our economic system makes it difficult to succeed. I don't buy it. I don't believe people only concern themselves with short term stability because of a lack of faith in the job market. I believe most of those individuals use this thought process as a coping mechanism to deal with reality. Living in poor communities and lacking money needed to provide basic necessities is not the lifestyle most people prefer. They are not living there to prove a point to the government. Most of these people have faith in our economy, but struggle with personal issues. Our faith in economic stability is the reason we wait hours in line for the new iPhone, iPad, concert tickets, Black Friday sale and other wants we hold in high regard. Our faith in job security even shows up in private business and government matters. Whenever a bad U.S. jobs report comes out the stock market drops and the opposite is also true. Federal and state government creates policies based on job loss and growth rates each year. Another important factor is work culture. We do not prefer to be viewed as a rebel in our workplace; therefore, we choose to blend in with the culture around us. If most of our co-workers dress in suits, then we wear suits. Being surrounded by people that drive nice cars and live in big homes also has an effect on us. When the expectation is to work longer than an 8 hour shift then we stay longer. Working in an environment where most people eat at restaurants for lunch can create pressure to spend money compared to bringing food from home. Whatever the culture is at our workplace it almost always has an effect on us. How much we allow that culture to affect our spending habits will contribute to our financial well being.

Addictions are most prevalent in adulthood. We only need to follow our bank transactions for them to appear. When we were children the foundation for our addictions were built. They are fully revealed once we lose parental restrictions. While children may be able to repeat actions enough times to create habits, they are usually limited based on adult supervision. Most children are not capable of creating a lifestyle based on an addiction because they answer to several people. Adults can choose to fully indulge in whatever addiction he or she has with little regard for other people. In fact, many adults will use other adults to further their addictive needs. We are capable of being addicted to any and everything. It may be easy to identify a drug, alcohol, sex, car, money or music addiction, but there are so many more. What about food, traveling, shopping, playing video games, collecting and the countless other subtle addictions? Addictions require dependency and money is a resource to satisfy it. Our money habits reveal our addictions. How much we allow these addictions to control our actions is where we all differ. Similar to alcoholics, some people overcome their addiction while others don't. Either way our finances will be affected. If we spend too much money or too little how does that change our ability to feed this dependency? Thoughts like this occur daily and how we respond will determine our financial well being. If we respond by spending the majority of our money to satisfy this addiction, then we will probably have debt problems. Not all addictions are equal in expense, but we are capable of allowing inexpensive addictions to lead us into debt problems. Today, the average cost for a newly released album in the United States can be around $12.00; which usually doesn't consume the majority of an average paycheck. While the average American citizen may not purchase albums on a weekly basis, a person with a music addiction just might. This equates to $624.00 being spent on albums per year. Many of you reading this may think this is a small amount of money, but that depends on how much residual income a person has. If a person has $100.00 remaining after paying monthly expenses, he or she could increase residual income by 26% as a result of cutting album spending by 50 percent. People with inexpensive addictions face similar issues. It is easy to lose track of money spent on inexpensive items because it doesn't immediately impact on our ability to pay for needs. How is $20.00 going to keep me from being able to pay a $1,200.00 mortgage payment? This type of thinking can cause people to fall in debt instead of being able to save. People with expensive addictions like cars, houses and vacationing deal with the same problem. Many wealthy people find themselves drowning in debt because of an addiction to a wealthy lifestyle. People in this situation sometimes forget their money supply is not endless. Until change occurs they will struggle with debt. Limiting the power addictions have on our wallet will lead to less debt and more saving. But, first we must accept our addictions.

One of the most influential factors in adult financial decision making is the media. We've already dealt with how the media effects us as children, but it changes when we become adults. When we were children the media was a source for the unknown. We had a limited exposure to the world. As adults, the media usually doesn't introduce us to new concepts or ideas. The media becomes a catalyst for our addictions and desires. There is a reason after watching certain television programs or listening to radio ads we have an emotional response. Advertisers create ads for the purpose of creating an emotional response. They look for the best combination of emotional stimulation, time scheme, and product placement. Superbowl commercial spots cost millions per minute and marketers are willing to pay this price to influence our buying habits. We understand why businesses pay actors, singers, models and athletes to endorse their product. Marketers want to invest in an influential medium to stimulate consumption. Our buying habits prove we are driven by emotions more than rational thinking. How many times have we found ourselves questioning why we purchased something? Only after the purchase is made do we realize it began with some form of advertising? We ignored all the signs while shopping. The best place to begin examining the impact media advertising has on our buying habits is the closet. What brand dominates our shoe collection? Whose name is on the tag of the majority of our clothes? How many different designers are represented in our wardrobe? There are over one million clothing designers in the United States. But, only handfuls make their way into our closets. The next place to look for media influence is inside our refrigerator and cabinets. Our purchases will likely represent a small percentage of food and beverage producers. Most major corporations make their products more available than smaller competitors, but that is not the leading factor in our purchasing habits. If businesses could outperform their competitors simply through production rates, there would be no need to advertise. Some people will claim their lack of variety in purchases is due to personal preference. Those same people probably never tried similar products from different producers. Ask anyone that eats Kellogg's brand cereals if he or she has tried generic versions of the same cereals. The most common answer will be no. How can we honestly say we prefer the taste of one item compared to another when we haven't tried anything else? Even our music collection is influenced by marketing schemes. How many times have we disliked a song and found ourselves liking the same song after hearing hundreds of replays on the radio? How much of our music collection contains artist signed to a major record label? There is evidence of media influence outside of our homes too. Our automobile purchases display media influence. We purchase cars because they can go from 0 to 60 mph in 5 seconds, but will never take advantage of it. Smaller vehicles with better fuel efficiency dominate parking lots because of the increased message of practicality. We desire luxury vehicles meant for occasional use for our everyday travel needs. Only a few vehicles are accepted as a sign of financial success. They also happen to be the most sought after vehicles. The media is clearly impacting our financial decision making. The method to lessen its effect is simple. Watch less television and listen to less radio programming.

9

RENT VS MORTGAGE

We have all gotten advice at one time or another regarding paying rent or mortgage payments. Some people are against renting while others embrace it. Neither choice is always right or wrong. There are advantages and disadvantages with both choices. The final decision should be based on financial and lifestyle goals. We should think about how each choice will affect our long term financial goals, short term financial goals and overall lifestyle goals. Let's examine both from a short term perspective.

Renting is a good option for people that need to increase their money supply. The cost of living is usually cheaper than living in a mortgage based home and only requires a short term commitment. It is also a good short term option for people that are not able to immediately commit to a mortgage payment. Too many people believe renting is a wasteful because of the lack of ownership. One problem with this philosophy is its lack of recognition for today's economy. Houses are no longer an investment with guarantee returns. The housing market doesn't appear to be stabilizing for at least another two years. The majority of homes in the United States are not appreciating at more than 1 percent per year and mortgage loan rates are stable. Therefore; there isn't much risk in waiting an additional year to purchase a home. Eventually interest rates and home prices will go up, but the increase will occur quickly before stabilizing again. So the chances of missing out on lower interest rates will be limited to a few months. Another problem with this philosophy is the lack of recognition for the average mortgage loan payment structure. For the first several years of a 30 year mortgage loan, the majority of monthly payments are going towards interest. The mortgage loan balance will reduce slightly without additional payments. If paying $800 per month for rent allows the renter to save $500 per month, then an $800 monthly mortgage payment isn't more beneficial. How is the renter wasting their money if the majority of their potential mortgage payment does not bring them closer to ownership? Wouldn't it be better for the renter to rent an additional year and save more money for a larger down payment? A larger down payment would ensure a smaller mortgage loan payment and allow for more savings. That additional $6,000 towards a down payment would result in a $20 - $50 reduction in monthly mortgage payments. We are assuming the same interest rate is offered and property value do not increase more than 1% in one year. Where a person resides is also a factor in renting versus paying on a mortgage loan. Large urban cities like New York are filled with renters. New York lacks many opportunities to buy properties and it is extremely expensive. People searching for a short term residence in cities like New York are likely to discover the benefits of renting.

Renting is also a good short term option when the job market is struggling. The rate of job loss combined with the lack of job growth has put many people in a position to need less costly living arrangements. Therefore; having the flexibility to quickly relocate can be great for people experiencing a reduction in household income. It is also less expensive to leave a rental property because rental leases can be broken for minimal cost compared to defaulting on a mortgage loan. Foreclosing as a result of income reduction can affect credit history for several years. The negative impact of breaking rental leases are more short term. In these scenarios renters are able to recover from their losses faster than mortgage payers. There are some instances when a person going through a home foreclosure can experience some short term benefits. A short term loop hole has been created in the foreclosure process. The foreclosure process takes years to complete because of new legislation. People can stay in their home and not make mortgage payments. This does have some short term advantages because of the ability to save money, but will result in more long term disadvantages. People in this situation will likely be forced to pay high interest rates on any future loans and will have a difficult time obtaining another mortgage loan. Mortgaged homes do have some short term benefits for people with a large cash reserve and the immediate goal of obtaining properties. Investors can acquire property much cheaper today than in recent years. Being able to meet down payment requirements allows them to maximize investment opportunities. Fully financed mortgage loans are rarely offered because of new national lending guidelines. Most banks also follow less risky lending practices. Less people are capable of acquiring property through mortgage loans, while people with large cash reserves can acquire more. This is truly a buyer's market for the rich. Until the economy improves the opportunities for investors to acquire property will increase.

Some people choosing between renting and buying don't have short term financial goals because of long term financial ambitions. These individuals have many factors to consider when determining which option is better from a financial perspective. They must figure out when to stop renting and start buying. Renting for too long can result in losing an unnecessary percentage of lifetime earnings. Imagine how much money is lost when buying a desired home is possible, but a choice is made to continue renting. While it is understandable for a person to rent with the purpose of saving money, there is a point when renting becomes too costly. Rent usually increases annually and the cost can catch up with the expenses associated with buying a home. If enough money to make a down payment has been saved, then renting has become a luxury.

This is the point where renters must determine the purpose of renting. If the purpose is for financial gain then it is time to purchase a home. What financial purpose would there be in paying rent when purchasing an ideal home is affordable? The key words in this scenario are ideal and affordable. Homes that are not ideal are often upgraded through increased debt. This increase may overshadow the financial purpose for not renting and cause more long term debt. Ideal may not mean the same thing to all people, but it must be understood on an individual level. Some people may think a single family home is ideal, while others may prefer a duplex. First time home buyers may see an inexpensive home as ideal and others may not. How ideal is defined is very important, but knowing the true cost of purchasing an ideal home matters the most.

The answer to which choice is a better long term financial option always goes back to cost versus reward. How much money will renting subtract from personal income? What impact will mortgage payments have on household income? Interest paid on 30 year mortgage loans is often greater than the original mortgage loan amount. A mortgage loan and interest charges can devour more than half of lifetime earnings. If a person earns $1,000,000 between the ages of 24 – 54; how big of a mortgage loan would be needed to lose half of this income? A $250,000 mortgage with a 5 percent interest rate would almost get it done. In this very common scenario, almost half of the lifetime earnings are lost before additional household expenses are covered. It may have been a better idea to rent a little longer to avoid losing such a large percentage of personal income. But what about the appreciated value of the home? The value of the home would need to double to break even. That's too much of a gamble. Even the best homeowner can not completely control their home value. Factors such as crime, schools, neighborhood development and the job market are outside of individual control. Counting on a minimal

100 percent increase in home value is not realistic and will often
lead to future debt problems. Even the best bookie will tell you
that's a bad bet. Some people have taken this chance because of
their pursuit of a lifestyle.

How much are we willing to pay for a desired lifestyle? The
answer to this question is a major factor in determining our long
term financial well being. Yet, many of us do not think about this
factor when making purchases. We often focus on the rate in
which we can achieve our goals instead of the cost. Previous
generations had to work 20 plus years to obtain their lifestyle, but
we want it sooner. Some people call this the on demand mentality;
which can be attributed to technology and social changes. Others
say people are less patient. Whatever the reason may be, this
behavior often shows up in our home buying process.

Mortgages and rental leases are just mediums to help us reach our
lifestyle goals. But the pursuit of them often leads to financial
demise. We can observe this behavior when studying the housing
boom between the years of 2000 and 2007. Mortgage loan officers
were taking advantage of little federal regulation by offering
consumers loans they could not afford. Some of these loans were
subprime loans without fixed interest rates. They allowed
consumers to pay smaller than usual mortgage payments before
having to make higher unaffordable payments. This period of
lower payments typically lasted between 5 and 7 years. Potential
buyers were being told to ignore their fears of higher payments.
They could simply resell or refinance the mortgage loan before
payments increased. The problem with those promises was the lack
of a guarantee. The risk involved was also understated. But, many
of us were not concerned with the risk either. We either ignored
the risk or put too much faith in the honesty of someone profiting
from our loans. The opportunity to obtain our lifestyle desires
outweighed the risk. The result was a nationwide mortgage crisis
which has yet to be overcome. We must value our long term

financial stability to avoid these long term mistakes. Are a few years of luxury worth a lifetime of debt? Some people would answer yes, but I am certain they are a minority. There are ways to take advantage of these mediums instead of allowing them to bury us in debt. Paying off mortgage loans within 15 years greatly diminishes potential income losses due to interest charges. It also increases the likelihood of true home ownership. The best feeling someone can get while closing on a home sale is to receive a check for all the proceeds of the home sale. All that stands in the way of this delightful moment is a mortgage company waiting for their share. The only way to prevent this from happening is to own all rights to the home being sold. Unfortunately, many of us obtain mortgages and never own the property. A mortgage loan is suppose to be a temporary solution to a short term problem; the inability to fully purchase a home. To take advantage of this short term solution we must not allow it to become a long term option. How much money is saved when we fully own a home and use it to obtain our next home? We could sell or rent our property and keep all of the profits. Those profits can be used for the next home purchase. This would result in less money going towards interest charges and retaining more income. It also increases the likelihood of obtaining our lifestyle dreams. Renting should result in a similar outcome. If renting consumes the majority of our income, then we won't be able to save money. Is renting in the Soho district of Manhattan worth the risk of eviction and small savings growth? A luxurious lifestyle may have seemingly been obtained, but how long can it be maintained. Is it worth the inability to purchase a home? The renter really hasn't reached his or her lifestyle goal. The renter is a pretender and aspires to afford this lifestyle. Until the desired lifestyle is affordable it is just a life goal. The goal is truly achieved once it is either possible to purchase the home or renting is an affordable luxury. It is pretty difficult to achieve this goal without being able to save money. Renters should keep all the advantages that come with renting. They should never give them up in pursuit of a lifestyle. This is how we truly take advantage of renting.

RENT VS MORTGAGE

10

HOMEOWNERSHIP IN YOUR 20's, 30's AND 40's

Many people are taught they have to be 50 or older to purchase a home without a mortgage loan. They are lead to believe a mortgage loan is necessary to obtain a home unless they fall into a large sum of money. Saving money for a full purchase is viewed as unrealistic for most people under the age of 40. These are ridiculously false claims and many people don't realize they believe in them. If it were otherwise, more people would be mortgage free home owners. Why else would mortgage loans be the preferred method of gaining home ownership? This perception creates wealth for a few and causes many more to drown in debt. It is very possible to become a home owner very early in our adulthood. To make this happen we need to change our perception of home ownership.

If we are able to avoid debt traps, then we will be in a great position to own a home before 30. Avoiding car loans, credit card debt, high student loans and any other personal loans will leave us with a lot of residual income. I am sure if some of you skipped a few chapters this appears unrealistic, but it really isn't that farfetched. Avoiding these debts before our mid-twenties is possible. Here is an example. Jasmine purchased her first car with money she made while attending high school and kept it through college. The car wasn't her ideal choice but did provide her with the transportation she needed. She comes from an average income household and had to attend community college for two years before switching to a four year university. While attending community college, Jasmine maintained a 3.75 GPA. Her grades enabled her to obtain a 2 year full scholarship to a local university. She successfully interviewed for an internship during her senior year and was offered a position upon graduating. The job came with full medical benefits and a $35,000 annual salary. After graduating with a bachelor's degree, Jasmine accepted the job offer from her internship and moved back home with her parents. While living with her parents, she agreed to contribute $250 per month towards household bills for twelve months. She also agreed to move out after this twelve month period expired. By creating this temporary living arrangement Jasmine's monthly expenses were $954 after gas, shopping, eating out, car insurance and cell phone expenses were accounted for. This living arrangement allowed Jasmine to save $1,000 per month until she was able to find an apartment. After living with her parents for twelve months she was able to move into a 1 bedroom apartment near her job. Her rent was $800 per month. After making an $800 deposit she used $9,600 of her saving to pay off her one year lease in advance. Her monthly expenses remained $954 after using the $250 she was paying her parents to cover utility expenses. Staying within this budget for the entire year allowed Jasmine to save $13,000. The remaining portion of her savings was spent on a few auto repairs and buying gifts for family and friends. She also decided to renew her lease another 4 years for an additional $100 per month. Over the next four years Jasmine was able to save an additional $20,000.ashe was able to do this because of her budgeting and annual merit raises. During this time, she also purchased a $15,000 car. Jasmine was able to do by using her savings and trading in her older car. Jasmine is now 25 and has no debt. She has$35,000 in savings and owns a car worth $11,000. In another four years, she could increase her savings to $85,000. All she would need to do is maintain her raise rate and not increase her living expenses by more than three percent annually. Good investment choices could allow her to save even more. By age 29, Jasmine can purchase her first home with little or no financing. While $85,000 may not enable all people to purchase the same type of home; it is generally enough money to purchase a home in any state. Is being a single adult with no children realistic for a 29 year old? It is becoming more common than many people realize. Unlike previous generations many people are deciding to have children and get married at older ages. The average age of married women and men has increased by at least ten percent over the past fifteen years. A lot of this can be attributed to an increased rate of women pursuing college degrees and entering the workforce. Changes in social norms have also contributed to this behavior. What about people with children or a spouse? Having a family can actually increase the potential of home ownership before 30. Let's go back to Jasmine at age 25 and add some of different variables. At this point in her life, she has $35,000 in savings and decides to marry her boyfriend Sam. They had been dating for four years. Sam has his own apartment and they decide to move into a new two bedroom apartment. Sam earns $40,000 per year and doesn't have much debt. He pays a $200 monthly car note and has a few small balance credit cards. Their new apartment comes with a $1,200 rent payment and provides more room for their growing family. Within a few months, Jasmine becomes pregnant and is scheduled to give birth shortly after her 26th birthday. How can this family possible save to purchase a house before 30? Well, let's look at the numbers. Before the baby is born, Jasmine and Sam expenses total $2,655 per month. Their monthly bills are as follows: $1,200 rent, $250 auto insurance, $200 car loan, $150 cell phone, $80 cable, $225 groceries, $100 electricity, $200 gas, and $250 miscellaneous. Their combined net income is roughly $4,913. Their monthly residual income is $2,258. Once the baby arrived, their monthly residual income was reduced to $1,100.00. For the next three years, this family would be able to save roughly $35,000 in addition to the $35,000 Jasmine already had in savings. These figures are adjusted for yearly inflation and do not include any interest gained from their savings. We are also assuming Sam had no savings before he and Jasmine got married. With all these variables, Jasmine would still be able to purchase a home. Sam and Jasmine did not have a combined six figure salary. They did not win the lottery or inherit thousands of dollars. They didn't save every dollar they earned. Neither one of them won a million dollar lawsuit. She didn't invest in the hottest stock on Wallstreet. The only requirements were a budget and dedication to reaching a goal. I am not under the illusion that $80,000 - &110,000 will be enough money to purchase a dream home. But, owning a home makes it easier to obtain dream homes. In both examples Jasmine was able to save $70,000 - $110,000 within nine years. Can you imagine what she would be able to do in another nine years? She would probably see at least another 15% increase in her salary and have a minimal net worth of $275,000. Jasmine could own her ideal home before she turns forty. How many people do you know in their late 30's that own their ideal home without a mortgage loan? Not many. The reason has everything to do with perception instead of ability. Good financial management during young adulthood usually results in future long term rewards. There is still hope for individuals those dealing with debt problems. It is never too late to overcome prior financial mistakes. The recovering begins with a paradigm shift. Debt can no longer be an excuse for a lack of progression. The key is to get back to zero or as close as possible. The zero I'm referring to is a state of little or no debt. People with debt problems that aspire to own a home must return to a previous financial state. They must return to their early adulthood. Before all the mortgages, car notes, student loans and credit cards balances. Age does not matter. This will work for a 20,

30, 40 or 50 years old. The journey towards a path of complete home ownership begins at zero.

11

MARRIAGE CHILDREN AND MONEY

The value of family cannot be measured in any currency or denomination. Our family members are invaluable despite any disagreements or small arguments we have with them. Whether we like them or not, our family members are an essential part of our lives. What we can measure is the cost of family. The reason our twenties and early thirties are the largest debt building period of our adulthood is because we are usually building a family. Many of our debt problems began when we were preparing for family life. A small apartment was no longer feasible for an expanding family. The sports car was not large enough for a baby seat and growing children. The old neighborhood didn't have good enough schools or wasn't safe enough to raise a family. Our wedding had to be grand and luxurious. We had to take a once in a lifetime vacation for our honeymoon. The wedding rings needed to be the biggest and best. All of these desires come with a hefty price tag and many of us are not prepared to pay for it. Paying attention to the cost of these life changing events can reveal its true cost.

The cost of marriage depends on many different variables. Let's start with money personalities. There are four classifications most people fall under when it comes to their money personality; chaser, builder, manager, and victim. Chasers are people that consistently attempt to acquire more wealth than someone else. These individuals perceive life as a race where first place is the only winner. This results in more financial risks being taken. They determine their level of success based on the failures of others. They also have a high regard for social status. People like Bill Gates and Warren Buffet are used for barometers of success. They may often be heard saying, "I haven't made it because I'm still not on the level of….." People with this money personality will often relocate more often than others. Their insistence on social advancement will not allow them to live comfortably in one setting for a long period of time. Builders desire to increase everything they acquire. These individuals may be considered rich, but want to expand their assets as much as possible. They perceive life as an individual race with the goal of beating an ever changing best time. They may often be heard using the phrase, "I am working to expand my empire." These individual are semi stable, but relocate more often than managers or victims. Managers desire to manage their earnings to the best of their ability. Income level is not a major concern. They are inspired to advance in their career, but not solely for the purpose of earning more money. Preparation and effort are highly regarded values to manager personalities. They use phrases like, "As long as I do my part everything else will fall in place." These people are less likely to frequently relocate and usually live a more stable lifestyle. Victims consistently blame their personal failures on others and circumstances. These individuals are not willing to do what it takes to change their circumstances. They often perceive life as a fixed race. They feel this race cannot be won without cheating. You may often hear them say, "It's not my fault." They are semi-risky partners because of their lack of desire to change. Victims may complain about their lifestyle, but will not take advantage good opportunities. These habits make victims a difficult spouse to live with. A good way to determine if living with a victim is possible is to understand financial compatibility. Some money personalities are better matches than others. Chasers and victims will usually have the most difficult time becoming compatible. They are financial opposites and frequently find themselves working against each other. Builders will have the same issues with victims. Imagine one spouse working ten hours a day while the other gambles all their savings away. To make matters worse, he or she doesn't want to work. Another difficult match for chasers are managers. It is pretty difficult for one spouse to manage household finances while the other risks all their savings with costly investments. Builders would be the better choice for chasers because of their similarities. They both want to increase what they have but their motivation is different. Managers prefer stability over unpredictable financial behavior. Managers are more compatible with victims because of their predictability. Victims may lose money due to gambling, but won't take too much of a financial risk. Managers and builders are also a good match because of predictability. Builders may want to expand their wealth, but are usually less risky than chasers. Of course not all people fall under a single money personality, but one trait is usually more dominate than the other. Financial personality traits can also be a good indicator of future lifestyle expenses. Chasers tend to be the most expensive partners. Their aspirations for higher status come with a hefty price tag. They must have the best cloths, cars, jewelry, and other material possessions even if it isn't affordable. Expensive travel and social events are also preferred by chasers. The goal may be to increase their wealth but they need to appear wealthy during the process. Builders are the second most expensive partners because of their desire for increase. They may not appear flashy but do prefer to take some risk to expand their empire. Three bedroom single family homes in a middle class suburb will not be enough to satisfy their long term lifestyle desires. Eventually there will be a request for a bigger house and more land. Victims are the third most expensive partners because of the potential money losses. These people are famous for spending money for goals they will rarely achieve. They take college courses but never obtain a degree. The professors or institution are always the reason for their failure. Victims pay for self-improvement guides but never read the information. They can't find a job because the hiring manager is always bias. Their lack of follow through will always be dismissed by an excuse and those investments will never turn into profit. This is the costly behavior of people with a victim personality. The least expensive partners are usually managers. Their lack of risk taking may cost the family some potential income, but will prevent frequent bad financial decisions from occurring. Many divorcees never realized they were so financially incompatible with their former spouse until it was too late. Better knowledge of their spouses' financial personality may have prevented marriage or divorce. We all have certain expectations coming into a marriage, but understanding money personalities help to create a more realistic perspective. Even the most financially incompatible partners can become more compatible once each person has a proper perspective. Money personality is not the only factor to consider when considering marriage What about the family?

Marriages are affected by family members. We all have very complex relationships with our family members and they affect every marriage. Some people keep their personal matters away from family members and others don't. These differences are often based on the financial structure of each household. There are four financial structures most families fall under; intra-household, multi-household, generational, and total inclusion. Intra-Household families share financial gains and losses exclusively with household members. These families do not consider people outside of their household in financial decision making. Outside family members may receive gifts, but there is no regard for their financial well being. Spouses from this family structure usually bring minimal family expenses to the marriage. When family members outside of the home need financial assistance they will not attempt to assistance. Multi-Household families share their financial gains and losses with some family members. They consider some family members in their financial decision making, but will purposely exclude others. This behavior occurs for several reasons. The most frequent cause is a strained relationship. Changes in these relationships also move family members in and out of this structure. Some family members may remain a consistent part of financial planning, while other may not. Uncle Jeff may be considered this month and not considered in the future. These families must consistently discuss family financial issues because of frequent changes. They have a wide range of expenses to discuss and it is important to be prepared. Generational families share financial gains and losses based on generation. This is usually determined by average age between mother and child. There is a consistent vertical movement of assets and debts. Siblings will not consider each other in financial decisions, but include all nieces and nephews. Parents look to their children for assistance as they grow older. The next generation is always the focus and estates are often left in their care. People from this family structure bring consistent family expenses to their marriage. They can calculate how much their family members will affect the household income more easily than others. The reason is because there are a set number of family members to consider. The dynamics of multi-household families consistently change, but generational families are more stable. They only change financial plans based on births and deaths. Unlike the generational model, total Inclusive families share financial gains and losses with all family members. Bloodline is the usual method of determining membership and this practice is commonly found within royal families. Their goal is to ensure all family members are financially stable. They do this to maintain some level of high social status or guarantee a long lasting lineage. Spouses in this family usually bring expenses based on family wealth. If they come from poor families then expenses will be very high. If they come from wealthy families then family expenses will usually be lower. Marriages fail and succeed based on the understanding of these financial structures. When couples understand their money personality and structure, they are better fit for future financial challenges. Credit reports only give people a snapshot of financial habits. These methods are better indicators of long term behaviors. The cost of getting married must also be addressed.

Weddings are not cheap. There are a few exceptions like Vegas style weddings or ceremonies with only a handful of people, but most weddings are much larger. These large weddings are very expensive. How can we not desire a grand wedding? Early in our lives we are constantly told our wedding day should be magical. This is the day most women have been looking forward to. Weddings fulfill a little girl's dream of being a princess for the day. It gives a young man the opportunity to watch his beautiful queen walk down the aisle to become his forever. This is the stuff movies are made of and we are sold this dream for decades. Many of us go for the big expensive wedding. Years later we regret it. We could've done so much with that money. We often ask ourselves, "Was it really worth it?" The answer is often based on long term financial impacts. Some people accumulate serious debt for their wedding date. Others refuse to spend more than one weeks pay on their wedding. So which choice is better? The answer is very personal and I will not attempt to define the value of a wedding day. What I will attempt to do is create more informed decisions. The first step in choosing what type of wedding to have is to understand the cost and how it will affect financial stability. Here are some wedding expenses to consider: Ceremony location, Ceremony Officiator, Ceremony decorations, Flowers, Limo Rental, Wedding Planner, Wedding Dress, Veil, Tuxedo, Suit, Musicians/Soloist, Photographer/Videographer, Programs, Gifts and Favors, Invitations, Guestbook, Thank You Cards, Beauty and Spa services, Wedding Rings, Reception Location, Reception Food Services, Reception Bar Services, Reception Decorations, Wedding Cake/Desert, will add up quickly. The final total can easily exceed $20,000.This is before the honeymoon cost are added. How much these expense will affect financial stability depends on available money. It is an American tradition for the parents of the bride and groom to pay for the majority of these expenses. But, this is never guaranteed. The Baby-Boomers are struggling with retiring in our current economy and are not positioned to assist with these expenses like in the past. Their savings and 401k's are being depleted daily. So how do you pay for a dream wedding with minimal parental assistance? There is one group that is more than willing to assist with this dilemma; banks. This is when decisions must be made. How much is this wedding worth? What percentage of life term earnings should be loss? If securing loans to finance your wedding is not possible, then the decision is easy. There is nothing to give up. However; people that can be approved for loans have a more difficult decision. Here is something to think about while making that decision. Most divorces can be attributed to money problems. Wedding debts linger on for years and can create a need for additional loans. These funds are needed to cover other normal life expenses. That could've been money for a newer car, private school, auto repairs, vacations and an overall better quality of life. The choice comes down to risking the stability of your marriage or having a grand wedding. I would go with the first option.

Getting married can mean gaining or losing some personal assets. Properties, automobiles, collectables and other personal valuables usually fluctuate to create one comfortable home. This new home requires getting rid of valuables and it is difficult to take a step back for the sake of another person. In spite of this feeling, we all must overcome them to create a new home. Nobody likes to feel left behind and this is a terrible way to start a marriage. To avoid doing this couples must first accept reality. While it may be ideal to find a spouse of equal financial stature, the opposite is more likely. The spouse that is further ahead will need to assist the other, but there should be a limit. Overcompensating for a spouse can cause more harm than good. How many loans have been taken to invest in failed projects? How often are old debts paid off by one spouse to only find them showing up again? What happens when one spouse stops working and was expected to go back to work? These are situations that can break marriages and need to be handled carefully. Money will not save relationships. It may be a good short term distraction, but will turn into a long term disaster. Problems will continue to grow while expensive vacations and luxurious jewelry is being purchased. Shopping trips will often be used to temporarily relieve deeper issues. People have even created lifestyles to avoid marital disputes. They will fill their schedules with activities to avoid interactions with their spouse. This doesn't require spending a lot of money, but the figures do add up over time. Some people don't participate in yoga classes, seminars, book clubs, martial arts and similar activities for personal growth. They are attempting to escape martial issues. When married people don't feel their ambitions are being considered, they will find ways to escape their disappointment. To avoid these types of scenarios, all couples must have a sound plan with defined long term goals. The spouse that is taking a step back will need reassurance for this actions and a plan is the best comforter. This is also effective for the spouse that needs to be helped because the plan will determine what is possible and what isn't. We don't like to feel less valuable than our spouse and mutually beneficial plans can remove animosity. Sustained marriages require combined aspirations. Working together to build a lifestyle will increase the likelihood of reaching financial freedom. Budgets will be more in sync and financial disputes will be minimalized. Problems arise when we bring all of our single aspirations to marriages. Our single dreams cannot remain our married dreams. If it does, then financial stability will always be a divisive issue.

Divorce is very costly. The entire process takes away personal financial freedom and emotional stability. This is the worst outcome of marriage. Two people come together to build a family and end up destroying each other's life. Unfortunately, the popularity of divorce has risen in the past decade. Today, almost 40 percent of marriages result in divorce. This is an all-time high for the United States and the trend isn't slowing down. How much these divorces will cost the people involved depends on individual circumstances. Some common expenses associated with the divorce process are attorney fees, court fees, appraisal fees, relocation cost, storage fees and therapy fees. Some people chose to bypass some of these expenses, but most are necessary. Hiring a good attorney can be the difference between long term financial hardship and a financial rebound. Money is the biggest dispute in divorce and each person will attempt to secure their financial stability. Child custody, alimony, assets and liabilities are typical tools used for this cause. People often walk away from divorces with more debt than they brought into the relationships. Others end up gaining more income. There are times when divorcees create mutually beneficial agreements, but this is rare. Disagreements about finances during a marriage typically don't result in monetary agreements within separation negotiations. Adjusting to post divorce lifestyles is also difficult. Two income households are easier to manage than single households. If one person losses work then the other can assist. Bills and leisure expenses can be split between two incomes. Child care costs are shared. Having to deal with these matters individually is a big adjustment. It requires a new way of thinking. The costs of all these adjustments are impossible to measure, but the effects are seen daily. Divorce may seem attractive to some, but the cost is rarely worth it.

Children are not cheap or expensive. They are a blessing to all families. Our lack of understanding the true cost of raising a child is what causes us to view children as expensive. How can a child be considered expensive when we make all decisions regarding their life? A child doesn't determine if he or she is born into a financially stable or unstable home. This is determined by the parents. Children don't decide where they will live or what school they will attend. They don't even decide if mommy and daddy will earn enough income to reasonable support the family. Children are bought into this world by their parents and they determine if raising their child will be expensive. This is why it is important to understand the cost of raising a child before having one. Unfortunately many of us cannot go back in time and change some of the bad financial decisions we made. But it is never too late to prepare for the cost of raising children. Let's begin with the costs associated with infants.

Immediately after leaving the hospital, certain infant needs must be addressed. The newborn needs a place to sleep, all medicines prescribed by a physician, food, clothing, pampers, cleansers, traveling seat and anything similar. They also need 24 hour supervision. These are only a few general descriptions of newborn needs and all the details within the descriptions are much more complex. The cost associated with these needs will vary based on product market, location, family, and government assistance. No matter what the cost; understanding these expenses within our community can better prepare parents to pay for them. Once a newborn has been home for a few months, many parents must transition some of their parental duties to a caretaker. Many employers offer their employees the opportunity to stay home with their newborns for a few months. Some will also distribute some level of compensation. Once this time period expires; these parents will need to have someone assist with the caretaking of their child. This assistance is commonly filled by daycare providers. All parents should research potential daycare providers at least one year in advance. They will likely be using this service for at least 3-4 years.

As newborns become toddler, they will need almost everything a newborn needs plus more. All bedding, pampers, clothing, shoes, foods, traveling seats, and similar needs will have to be updated to accommodate growth. These accommodations will be more expensive than before. Toddlers will also need new toys and more complex games to account for their increased intelligence. Number blocks and key rings are no longer enough. There are also other important changes taking place. During these years children will gain playmates and this will cause parents to occasionally accommodate for other toddlers. Adding a few dollars to the budget for other children is never a bad idea and should be practiced more frequently. Though children are going through many changes as toddlers, the next stage in their life presents more first time expenses. Preschoolers are very different from toddlers. They can communicate better and are more curious about the world that surrounds them. These children are at a stage where they need some form of education and parents have some very important decisions to make. Almost all parents want their children to have the best opportunity to excel in life. The medium to these opportunities usually come in the form of preschool or some similar learning center. This is where an important financial question must be answered. How much are we willing to pay for this medium? Some will pay as much as it takes to provide their children with the best education. Others will pay as much as they can reasonable afford. This choice will likely have a long lasting effect, but not only for the children. This decision often determines the financial well-being of the entire household. It is difficult to provide the best education for children and settle for less than the best later in their lives. The best schools have two things in common; high cost and addiction. Parents pay a high cost but don't want to send their children to underachieving schools. It is also difficult to pay more for schooling than we are comfortable with. Once adults become accustom to education fitting within their budget, it is never easy to change. When children leave the preschool phase of their lives they become a lot more complex.

Between the ages of 5-9 children will undergo rapid physical and mental advancements. Cheaper clothes will quickly become too small and need to be replaced by more expensive clothes. Shoes will also need consistent replacement. But the largest jump in expenses will be related to their social changes. During these years, children are more aware of the society around them and begin to develop their identity. They become involved in sports, music, afterschool programs, and many other extra-curricular activities. What do all these activities have in common? Most of them are not free. Parents need to be prepared for this financial change and adjust their budgets accordingly. This is also an age where children will want more expensive games and toys. Cries for dolls and cheap electronics will be replaced with calls for expensive video gaming systems. Peer pressure will drive them to consistently ask for the most popular clothes, toys and gadgets. The house will frequently become boring and demand for vacations/ family outings will increase. At this age, life is about the pursuit of fun and parents have to bear the cost. This is another critical point where financial decision must be made. How much money should parents spend to accommodate the wants of children? It was easier and cheaper to fulfill these wants when they were preschoolers. Most of their wants were inexpensive and they weren't so aware of the world around them. Unfortunately, those times will never return and how parents move forward will affect the household for years. Giving children whatever they want will likely cause financial problems and breed spoiled people. Not giving children enough can lead to resentment and cause them to look elsewhere for love. There is no perfect formula for all families to follow, but finding a happy medium is possible. Parents must understand their financial well being and commit to certain guidelines to be successful. Spending limits must be set and childhood behavior must be observed. It is important to establish this while they are younger. Once children become pre-teens, it may be too late.

Preteens are children between the ages of 10 and 12. Based on their numerical age this is a very short timeframe within childhood, but maturity levels may change at a faster pace. Some new expenses related to puberty will need to be addressed, but the biggest changes may be related to communication. By this time children will probably want a cell phone, if they don't already have one. They want to be in constant contact with their friends and the internet will not be enough. Many parents will also want their preteens to have a cell phone because of their concern for safety. Preteens spend more time away from the home than ever before. Parents are well aware of how dangerous this world can be and communication brings comfort. This combination of changes will result in higher cellular expenses. While preteen years are short, the next stage in childhood will last much longer and require more money.

Teenagers require a lot of attention and create a need for more intricate financial planning. Their wants are more expensive. They cost more to feed. Education expenses reach an all-time high. But most importantly; they are transitioning into adulthood. Let's begin with examining the effect on household grocery expenses. Teenagers eat a lot more than any other children in the household. They can eat as much as the parents or sometimes even more. Outside of food there will also be an increased desire for toiletries and other cosmetic items. Expect at least a 10% increase in grocery expenses. Clothes and shoes expenses will also see a sharp rise. This is a time period when children have a stronger desire for self-identification. Their wardrobe is affected by this behavior. Teenagers frequently change their appearance and their clothing is a lot more expensive than before. But, these changes are minor compared to the next set of new expenses. Most teens want to drive and adding a teenager to insurance plans is very costly. Parents should expect at least a 100% increase in their insurance rates once they add a teenager to their policy. Driving school and drivers test fees also will need to be addressed. Parents that allow their teens to drive should also expect an increase in auto repair expenses. New drivers do not excel at keeping cars spotless. Buying teenagers their own car also comes at a high cost. The parents' car commanded a little more respect and couldn't be used as frequently. On the other hand; their car has more accessibility and doesn't require the same level of respect. This behavior is to be expected of a teen and so should an increase in expenses. Extracurricular activity expenses will also rise. The cost of participating in class trips, field trips, school dances, proms, sports, school clubs, ring ceremonies, and similar activities will be higher than ever before. Somebody has to pay for the new football field and lab equipment. School officials can't realistically expect their students to cover all these expenses. That burden belongs to the parents. Next up is the expense all parents should be prepared for. Applying to and paying for post high school graduation aspirations. Before teenagers graduate from high school their next step should already be addressed. This is something that can't be held off until the last minute. Parents have 17 years to prepare for this moment and those that didn't will have some tough decisions to make. This is not a decision that only parents of children that will go to college must decide. Parents with children that do not attend college or leave home also have an important decision to make. How much longer will they bear the living expenses of their child? Other parents must deal with their child transitioning to college. Application fees and campus visit should be the least of all concerns. The most important matter will be paying for college after the acceptance letters are received. Parents of children with full scholarships can relax during this process because this expense will be addressed. Unfortunately, most parents won't have this luxury. These parents have an important decision to make. But, they shouldn't be too worried. This decision was made a long time ago, when the children were just preschoolers. Some parents decided to save for school and others didn't. Some decided to pay any price for education. Others choose affordable education options. The decisions made then will usually be the same decisions made now.

MARRIAGE CHILDREN AND MONEY

12

RETIREMENT

I told my wife when we first got married I wanted to retire in my 40's. She looked at me as if I were crazy and quickly dismissed my foolish comment. I couldn't blame her either. It sounds so unrealistic to expect retirement at such an early age. But is it really unrealistic? Based on today's economy it would seem so, but that doesn't mean it isn't possible. Why strive towards financial freedom if the goal isn't to enjoy retirement? Debt is what hinders these ambitions. Cost of living expenses combined with wealth disparity has led many seniors to continue working well past 62. This is the age we qualify for social security payments, but not full retirement benefits. Full retirement age had been 65 for many years. However, this age has increased. People born after 1959 are not considered of full retirement age until they are 67 years old, according to the SSA. The government must want us to work and pay taxes a little longer than before. They are in debt to our social security fund. But, they are not the problem. Many finance experts blame bad retirement strategies for prolonged retirement. But, complex investment plans are not necessary for retirement. The biggest reason we don't retire at an earlier age is DEBT; plain and simple. We give away too much of our lifetime earnings. Our sixties should be filled with travel and life changing experiences. We need to be celebrating our lifetime achievements and looking back at them with laughter. Unfortunately, many of us left this path a long time ago.

With the baby- boomers next on deck for retirement, things are not looking too good. They were told retirement would be easy if they had IRA and 401k savings. Sadly, many 401k and IRA accounts have been depleted because of the Great Recession. According to an AARP study, 25 percent of people ages 46 to 64 say they have no retirement savings. 22 percent over the age of 65 say the same thing. Their plan was to use these savings accounts to pay off mortgage loans and all other debts. This would allow them to retire with ease. The problem with this expectation is the overvaluing of 401k and IRA plans. These accounts alone cannot guarantee successful retirement. No plan should ever encourage people to carry long term debt. Retirement and mortgage payments do not mix. Retirees with no mortgage payment pay thousands less for their monthly expenses; despite where they live. Mortgage debt has created a need for retirees to maintain 80 to 100 percent of preretirement income levels. It was closer to 70 percent about ten years ago. This income level is not realistic for most retirees. Compared to the early 1990's, the debt level of seniors is five times higher. The majority of this increase is directly related to mortgages. Home sales have been down for the last five years and seniors are having a hard time getting out of their mortgage loans. Those unable to sell their homes often take second mortgages to increase their money supply. Medical expenses are high for all seniors and they need to pay for their prescriptions. Credit cards and auto loans also contribute to this problem. All these debts eventually snowball and cause serious hardships. This debt consumption is prolonging retirement. Seniors are struggling to retire at an age when their bodies are failing. They are working longer and passing on more debt than assets. But, there are ways to slowly down this trend.

The best way to make sure this doesn't happen is to have good preparations. The earlier we start to prepare for our retirement, the better chances we have to retire before 65. Some resources people use to build savings for their retirement are 401k's, IRA's (Roth and traditional), 403b's (mostly tax-exempt organizations) and

457's. 401k savings are the most popular retirement planning investment accounts used by employers in the United States. Employees have a great amount of control over their contribution percentages and investment packages. These packages are usually mutual funds with a mixture of bonds, stocks, money market investments and company stock. Contributors can begin to withdraw funds from these accounts at 59 ½ without any penalties. 403b savings accounts are very similar to 401k plans except they are only offered to tax exempt organizations like schools. 457 savings accounts are similar to 401k plans but there are no penalties for withdrawing funds before 59 ½. Contributing to these accounts is better than not saving at all. Still, there is more work needed for retirement. Managing debt is just as important as saving money. Effective management of debt requires paying close attention to lifestyle choices. A safe lifetime debt to income ratio is 30 percent. When debt levels exceed 36 percent of total household income; the likelihood of financial hardship increases significantly. It is possible to get a mortgage loan at a 41 percent debt to income ratio, but long term financial stability requires less debt. Most lenders consider debt to income ratios above 35 percent to be unsustainable. These debt levels are more risky is because they create more vulnerability to monetary emergencies. Unexpected emergencies can be very expensive and can cause big problems for people with high debt levels. These emergencies will slow down the ability to prepare for retirement and lead to working longer than expected. Retirement is something too many people overlook before the age of 50 and the consequences are devastating. To avoid these hardships we must limit debt growth during the latter years of life.

If you are not convinced of the ability to retire before the age of 60, let me show you how realistic it is. Let's continue to follow the life of our favorite character, Jasmine. By age 39, Jasmine's minimum net worth is $275,000. She has no mortgage and little debts. Her children went to college, but both accumulated minimum debt. One child received enough scholarships to fund her education. Her other child went to community college and transferred to a four year university with a two year scholarship. If she maintains her level of savings, she will be able to save at least $500,000 over 15 years. How is this possible? Jasmine would need to save roughly $30,000 per year. She was saving at this rate in her 30's. We can do amazing things when mortgage debt and credit card debt is removed. Jasmine's minimum net worth would be $775,000 at the age of 54. She could pay herself $20,000 for the next 25 years. This is without social security or any retirement funds. Jasmine could live without using these sources of income through age 79, unless she lives in an expensive city like LA or NY. If her husband matches these efforts they will have a combined net worth of 1.3 million by age 54. Pensions, 401'ks, IRA's and social security income should eventually add at least an additional $24,000 per year for each person. This is based on Jasmine and her husband earning $50,000 each per year. At this pay rate, contributing a company matched 5% of their income to a 401k would equate to $10,000 per year. In 15 years these saving would be at least $150,000. That increases their net worth to 1.45 million at age 54. This is not accounting for any increases in pay or positive investment performance. I wouldn't recommend them to retire at the age of 54, but it would be possible in most cities.

13

WHAT IF I'M ALREADY IN DEBT HOW DO I GET OUT?

Paying off debt requires commitment and consistency. Halfhearted efforts will lead to consistent failures and debt problems will persist. This has been proven true time and time again. It happens to the national government and American households. Some people have chosen to ignore this fact instead of accepting the truth. When celebrities file for personal bankruptcy; debt problems were ignored. When millionaires lose their homes to foreclosure; debt problems were ignored. When national governments balance sheets are in the red; debt was ignored. Time and time again debt has been ignored and allowed to flourish, but this doesn't have to happen. To really overcome bad money habits a paradigm shift must occur. There must be a high regard for financial wellbeing and it must be protected by any legal means necessary. This process begins when debt problems are fully accepted. The previous chapters have dealt with the contributors to debt problems. Blaming circumstances and people for debt issues must stop. The debt belongs to whomever name it is listed under, despite the reasons it exist. Either accept it or be willing to live with the consequences. Those willing to accept their debt problems should read on. All others are wasting their time.

A wise man once told me, "If we fail to plan then we plan to fail". Overcoming debt problems requires planning. The chances of overcoming debt due to an unexpected windfall of money are slim to none. Therefore, the majority of us will need a plan. So where do we begin? First we must identify all of our debts. For many of us that ignored our debt, this may take some hard work, but it is possible. A few tools that can assist with identifying debt are credit reports, caller id, saved mail, emails and old voicemails. Credit reports enable us to identify the majority of our debts. These reports list all debts reported by lenders and provide creditor contact information. The three major agencies that provide these reports are Trans Union, Experian, and Equifax. It is important to use credit reports from all three major credit bureau reporting agencies because they differ. All creditors do not report to the same agency. Having all three guarantees the ability to identify all debts. Caller ID can also be used to gather collector contact information. We all have ignored calls from 800 numbers and out of state numbers at some point in our lives. When we are in debt these numbers are avoided like the black plague, but they are useful while paying off debt. Calling a few of these numbers back can help us identify debt. Old debts are often sold to collection agencies and recent calls can lead us to the current owner. During these calls most collectors will attempt to collect on the debt, but that will be done later. Remember, we are only locating our debt at this stage. Looking for current and old mail will also help to tally up the bills. When we have debt problems, many of us will never open mail. We don't want to be reminded of our problems. Well, now is the time to stop ignoring the bills. Opening the mail will help us to find the most up to date information in regards to our debt. We change our phone numbers more often than we change our residence. Lastly; emails and saved voicemails are good tools to round up our debt. Most creditors ask for email information when we apply for loans and it is stored in their files. Those emails are used for collection activities, therefore; our email inboxes are a great place to identify outstanding debts. Just like mail, voicemails often house messages from creditors. Listening to these old messages will yield some good information, if there is no other way to identify who owns our debt. When all of our debt information has been collected, then we can begin to create a debt reduction plan.

This stage of debt reduction planning is very overwhelming. A list of our debts can seem insurmountable and unbearable and cause us to flee plan creation. We must overcome this feeling to move forward. Fear and stress keeps too many people from fixing their financial problems. We can overcome debts and this plan will help us to get there. We will begin with accurately accounting for our income.

When listing our income, we must exclude any money that is not guaranteed. Technically none of our paychecks are guaranteed, but this refers to money outside of regular income. Scratch off the yearly bonuses, monthly incentives, gambling winnings and any other irregular source of income. Minimalizing our income will provide the most leverage. All plans need room for mistakes and unexpected expenses.

Next we need to prioritize our expenses. The mandatory expenses are rent, food, water, utilities, prescriptions, transportation, minimal communication, insurance, clothing, school supplies and housing. These are must haves and we should be able to pay for these expenses. If paying for these expenses is not possible, this is where most of the planning will begin. This situation requires a drastic change in lifestyle. To address this situation we must find additional household income or a less expensive residence. The first option is not a guarantee. It requires us to either find an additional revenue generating housemate or obtain another consistent source of income. The likely of finding either depends on proximity to eviction. Two months or less may not be enough time to find a roommate. Eviction mandates the second option. Finding a less expensive home may be the easier option, but there are potential negative side effects. More affordable living options may be in crime filled neighborhoods with underachieving schools. Unfortunately, this may be the only option. There is some upside to this move. It will provide the best opportunity to overcome all debt problems and increase the likelihood of achieving financial freedom.

Once our monthly needs are accounted for, we must deal with the other expenses. These are our student loans, credit cards, personal loans, cable contracts, internet service agreements, cell phone bills, overdue taxes, collection accounts, overdue medical bills and other similar expenses. To begin we must identify which of these expenses require minimal effort to reduce. This means stopping all cable/satellite services, cell phone services, gym memberships, magazine subscriptions, internet services, newspaper subscriptions and other luxuries we really can't afford. When we call to stop these services, we cannot allow customer service representatives to change our mind. They will offer us everything in the world to keep our business with them, but it isn't enough. Discounts will not help. Stopping these services is the only way to move forward. There is no room for short cuts. The goal at this stage is to free up as much money as possible.

After luxury expenses are minimalized, we can work on reducing reoccurring monthly expenses. Bills that are possible to adjust need to be addressed first. These are monthly expenses that can be lowered by working with creditors. Credit card, automotive and personal loan lenders are most willing to negotiate payment plans. This process doesn't require a bachelor's degree in finance or communication. We need to be honest about our financial hardship and recognize where leverage is present. Collectors need our payments to keep their job. The goal is to create a beneficial arrangement for all parties. If collectors are unwilling to offer payment plans, then try other tactics. Ask to speak to a supervisor or callback another day. These conversations should free up some of our cash flow, but we must avoid unnecessarily extending any loans. Adding additional years to a loan can be detrimental to this process. There is no need to adjust any bills that will be paid off within one year. Loans with more than one year terms can be extended if necessary.

The last step in this part of the process is to identify which monthly expenses to pay off first. Debts that can be paid off the fastest should be paid first. These are debts with low balances and high payments. Loans with identical balances should be prioritized based on monthly payments. The highest payment should be paid off first. This type of payoff plan requires aggressive payments. Paying 5 dollars above the minimum payment is not aggressive. Payments need to be increased by at least 25 percent. If this isn't possible then it is ok to add less. The money we gained from cutting back on luxury services and reducing loan payments should help with this effort. If there is money left over after this new pay down plan is implemented, then use it wisely. I would recommend either paying another bill or building up a small savings for emergency expenses. These efforts create more residual income and lessening our dependency of credit. Once one reoccurring monthly expense is paid off, we must repeat the same steps with another. The ability to do this with all of our monthly expenses is difficult but realistic. Knocking off one debt at a time will eventually lead to eliminating all debts. Next up on the chopping block; collections and charged off accounts.

GETTING OUT OF DEBT

MONTHLY BUDGET

MONTHLY INCOME
MONTHLY INCOME AFTER TAXES_____
MONTHLY INVESTMENT INCOME_____
MONTHLY INTEREST INCOME_____
TOTAL MONTHLY INCOME_____

MONTHLY EXPENSES

LOAN EXPENSES	**EDUCATION EXPENSES**
MORTGAGES_____	TUITION_____
AUTO LOANS_____	FEES_____
SCHOOL LOANS_____	SUPPLIES_____
PERSONAL LOANS_____	BOOKS_____
CREDIT CARDS_____	OTHER_____
TOTAL LOANS_____	**TOTAL EDUCATION**_____

SERVICE EXPENSES

GAS & ELECTRIC_____	HAIR/SKIN CARE_____
WATER_____	DAYCARE_____
TRASH PICKUP_____	BABYSITTING_____
SEWAGE REMOVAL_____	INTERNET _____
GYM MEMBERSHIP_____	SECURITY_____
FITNESS INSTRUCTION_____	DRY CLEANING_____
ATHLETIC INSTRUCTION_____	CABLE/SATELITE_____
MUSIC LESSONS_____	HOME CLEANING_____
ACTING LESSONS_____	CELL/TELEPHONE_____
CHILD RELATED LESSONS_____	AUTO MAINTINANCE_____
MAGAZINE/NEWSPAPER_____	OTHER_____

TOTAL SERVICE EXPENSES_____

MEDICAL EXPENSES	**TRANSPORTATION EXPENSES**
DENTAL_____	GAS_____
VISION_____	.PUBLIC TRANS_____
MEDICAL_____	INSURANCE_____
THERAPUDIC_____	TOLLS_____
COSMETIC_____	RENTAL_____
OTHER_____	OTHER_____
TOTAL MEDICAL_____	**TOTAL TRANS**_____

FOOD/HOME EXPENSES	**CLOTHING/LEISURE EXPENSES**
GROCERIES_____.	CLOTHES SHOPPING_____
FAST FOOD_____	OTHER SHOPPING _____
FARMING_____	DATING_____
HOME INSURANCE_____	VACATIONS_____
OTHER_____.........	OTHER_____
TOTAL FOOD/HOME_____	**TOTAL**_____
TOTAL ALL EXPENSES_____	**TOTAL ALL INCOME**_____

PAY DOWN PLAN

TOTAL BALANCES OF DEBTS BEING PAID

_____   _____
_____   _____
_____   _____
_____   _____
_____   _____

TOTAL BALANCES OF DEBTS NOT BEING PAID (WITH
ORIGINAL LENDERS....NOT COLLECTIONS AGENCIES)

_____   _____
_____   _____
_____   _____
_____   _____
_____   _____

TOTAL BALANCES OF DEBTS NOT BEING PAID (COLLECTIONS
AGENCIES AND THIRD PARTIES)

_____   _____
_____   _____
_____   _____
_____   _____
_____   _____

DEBTS BEING PAID THAT CAN BE PAID OFF FASTEST

_____   _____
_____   _____

DEBTS NOT BEING PAID THAT CAN BE PAID OFF THE FASTEST

_____   _____
_____   _____
_____   _____

Dealing with collection agencies and law firms can be annoying, but it is necessary. All fears and concerns must be overcome. These collectors need us to pay our debts just as much as we need to pay them off. Collections agencies purchase our debts from the original lender and they want to make a profit from their purchase. We shouldn't avoid collectors just because of their attempts to intimidate us. The consequences of not dealing with these collectors can be far worse than simply speaking with them. We don't want to check our bank accounts and find out our hard earned money has been intercepted. Collectors are filing small claims lawsuits more than ever before. Not honoring a court summons results in either liens or even bench warrants. Many people have been pulled over by state troopers for speeding and ended up going to jail for failure to appear in court. This could put jobs and reputations at risk. Another bad choice is to hire someone to settle debts. The most common choice for representation is settlement agencies. Settlement agencies negotiate deals with collectors to lower debt balances. They claim to be able to lower overall debt by 20 to 50 percent and make sure all the harassing calls stop. Settlement companies claim to hire the best debt negotiators in the world. Their so called experts are trained to get the best deals. This sounds really good until all the fine print is revealed. They forget to tell potential customers how much of their money is being put aside for profits. There is no mention of the collectors' ability to file a lawsuit working with them. Settlement agents never tell customers they have no leverage when negotiating with collectors. Why would a third party have more leverage than the person responsible for the debt? This just doesn't make sense. They are really just an expensive middle man and can cause more harm than good. These are for profit organizations and they are not in business just to help people with debt problems. Unfortunately, many people find this out the hard way. Once an agreement is signed there is no turning back. Terminating a contract with most settlement agencies will not result in a full refund. There are some good organizations out there to help people going through financial problems and they usually have one thing in common. They are nonprofit organizations. These debt counseling service providers are partially funded by state or national government grants. They must adhere to strict guidelines to maintain their funding. The programs they offer are not free, but their fees are much less than the alternative. To ensure a debt counseling service is a good organization, it is recommended to do some research. Stay away from any organization with a high number of complaints. Ask friends and families if they have heard anything about these organizations. With enough research it will be easy to separate the good from the bad. If working with third party organizations is too much work, try to deal with collection agencies directly. Preparation must be done before contacting these companies. Never contact a collector without knowing how much money can be used to pay down or pay off the debt. Allowing collectors to determine payments can lead to broken arrangements. They won't fully understand all circumstances contributing to this debt. Be the first to offer a settlement and make sure the offer is not the best offer. Collectors often respond to an initial settlement offer with a lower offer. The lowest offers will be offered if they believe there is a serious financial hardship. Allowing collectors to make an initial settlement offer will also result in larger settlement agreements. The goal is to always get collectors to offer their very best. The best offers are presented when collectors believes there isn't much money available for the settlement. A good sign of their best offer is the need for additional signoff or managerial approval. Managers are required to sign off on the lowest offers. The battle doesn't end when the final settlement offer is accepted. There is one drawback to even the best settlement offer. Any settlement agreement resulting in forgiveness of more than $600 is considered taxable income. A 1099-c form will be sent for the year the settlement is paid. The only way to get out of paying taxes on this forgiven debt is to be considered insolvent; total debt exceeding total income. This will require a 982 tax form to be filled out and attached to the 1099-c form. A tax advisor can always assist with this process if needed. All settlement negotiations will not end with an agreement. Payment plans are another option if a settlement isn't possible, but the rules are the same. Go into the call understanding what is affordable. The amount of money to be distributed to each debt should already be determined. Deviating from this plan will only make things harder. The last resort is to pay the predetermined amount despite failed negotiations. Collections agencies will not turn down our money even if the payment is less than what they are requesting.

Filing bankruptcy should always be a last resort effort to deal with debt problems. Many people believe this is the easy way out of debt problems, but that is far from the truth. The process of filing bankruptcy is long and costly. Many steps must be taken and the aftermath is a terrible credit standing. To begin the bankruptcy process you must first decide if the services of an attorney will be retained. It is possible to file bankruptcy without an attorney, but this action can cause more problems. There is a lot of paperwork and procedures to follow. Doing this yourself increases the odds of something being missed. Retaining the services of an attorney is the easy but more expensive option. The average fee for filing bankruptcy is between $250 and $430, based on which chapter is filed. Chapter 7 bankruptcy is the most common filing because it allows all debts to be resolved without repayment. Chapter 13 bankruptcy is another option for filling, but there is a requirement to pay most debts in three to five years. No matter which filing is chosen the fee for an attorney is usually between $1,000 and $2,000. These fees must be paid before the actual case is filled and there are few exceptions. The hardships involved with this process don't end with the fees. You must prove the need for chapter 7 or chapter 13 bankruptcies, but most attorneys will determine this during an initial consultation. Mandatory debt counseling sessions are also required within the bankruptcy process. These courses must be completed before any bankruptcy is approved. The most significant outcome of filing bankruptcy is the effect on your credit. Bankruptcy filings stay on your credit report for 10 years. This gives every creditor the right to either turn down your credit applications or charge the highest possible interest rates. You've probably heard stories about people filing bankruptcy and getting a car loan the next year. You may have even heard of a person filing bankruptcy and getting a home loan 2 years later. But they never tell you at what cost they were able to get those loans. What about after the bankruptcy filing disappears from your credit report? Credit lenders are not so easily fooled. An empty credit report indicates either young age or previous bankruptcy filings. Most adults use credit by the age of 25. I've reviewed hundreds of credit files and never witnessed this behavior without a previous bankruptcy filing. Sure, some people never use credit, but they are a small minority. Filing bankruptcy isn't all negative. Collectors do go away and debt is liquidated. Any collector pursuing debt after bankruptcy is declared must be asking for a lawsuit. When there is no realistic way of turning around major debt problems this may be the only answer. A few thousand dollars is not worthy of bankruptcy, but fifty thousand could warrant filing. To make the best choice all options and outcomes must be considered. Getting back on the path of financial freedom requires some drastic changes. Bankruptcy can be the most uncomfortable option, but may be a necessary step. The goal is to lower debt though realistic methods.

Great plans are useless without proper execution. Not following through on plans will result in failure. How many weight loss plans have failed? How often do first time businesses fail within three years? Maximum effort is readily available in the beginning, but later in the process it dwindles away. This has occurred too often within financial planning, but there are ways to escape this cycle.

One method of staying consistent is to allow cheating within any financial plan. It is not realistic to expect every dollar to go towards paying down bills and saving. Who wants to work hard and never reap the rewards of their success? Financial freedom is the destination, but there are stops along the way. Creating space in your budget for entertainment, dates and other inexpensive activities is necessary. The key to doing this without overspending is to understand timing. There is a time to save for these activities and time to spend. The best way to these opportunities is to know your breaking point. The breaking point is when you stray away from your plan. The breaking point is the moment you buy something and realize afterwards it goes against everything you promised to do. This can occur after one week or several months. Long term success depends on the acceptance of this behavior. What do you do about this habit? Build it into the budget. Always save a small portion of your income for breaking points. Small portion don't take away from a true necessity. Small may not even equal 5 percent of you bi-weekly income. A small portion should be enough to allow minimum exposure to some form of entertainment. This adjustment should not extend your plan by more than one month. Here is a quick example. Erica brings home $1,000 every other week and pays $900 in expenses to stick to her debt reduction plan. In the past, she fell short of her plans because of the urge to spend with her hard earned money. She noticed this happens whenever she gets paid and decided to do end the trend. To make sure she did not totally fall off her plan, she decided reduced debt payments by $50 every other week. Erica has $200 per month to spend on whatever she wants. She made an adjustment and sticks to the plan. If she had reduced her plan by $300 or greater, the plan would've failed. Why? When plans are extended too far they usually fail.

Another way to ensure success is to create milestone incentives. Add rewards for cutting outstanding debts by $1,000 or increasing savings by $500. People may not like to admit it, but we all like to be paid for our accomplishments. Children get rewarded for good report card grades and grow into adults expecting rewards for hard work. This is the American way. You may find that incentives help to maintain the course. Using a virtual money tracker can also help. Some people need to physically see their debt reduce and money supply increase. There are hundreds of ways to do this using computer software and downloadable apps. These programs will allow you to have a visual picture of your success. They provide encouraging messages along this difficult journey. Every little bit helps. Any of these tools will increase the chances of completing your plan, but sometimes more drastic measures are needed.

Giving someone else control of your money is an extreme but very effective method of ensuring success. You may need someone to help control your bad habits. A close relative, friend or a financial institution can fill this need. A few factors to consider when choosing the right person are reliability, stubbornness, proximity and of course trustworthiness. The ideal person will be able to turn down your request for money. It takes a special person to keep your money from you and everyone is not built to handle this task. This person shouldn't be too accessible because there needs to be some level of inconvenience to deter frequent visits. If your helper lives 15 minutes away then there will be too many opportunities to ask for the money. Keep this person as far away as possible. Long distance also will require a lot of trust. You can't just give your money to anybody and expect him or her to not spend your money. This person must already be financially stable. Giving your money to someone that needs money is a recipe for disaster. No matter how honest they try to be, the temptation to temporarily borrow money will be too great. If you can't find anyone to fill this role, you may need to use a bank. Most banks offer several accounts that can assist with budgeting discipline. Certificate of Deposit accounts and high minimum balance accounts are capable of fulfilling this need. They penalize frequent withdrawals. Using a small out of state bank may also help to deter frequent usage.

EXAMPLE OF BREAKING POINT TRACKER

JANUARY

DAYS BEFORE BREAKING_____
WEEKS BEFORE BREAKING____

FEBRUARY

DAYS BEFORE BREAKING_____
WEEKS BEFORE BREAKING____

MARCH

DAYS BEFORE BREAKING_____
WEEKS BEFORE BREAKING____

APRIL

DAYS BEFORE BREAKING_____
WEEKS BEFORE BREAKING____

MAY

DAYS BEFORE BREAKING_____
WEEKS BEFORE BREAKING____

JUNE

DAYS BEFORE BREAKING_____
WEEKS BEFORE BREAKING____

JULY

DAYS BEFORE BREAKING_____
WEEKS BEFORE BREAKING____

AUGUST

DAYS BEFORE BREAKING_____
WEEKS BEFORE BREAKING____

SEPTEMBER

DAYS BEFORE BREAKING_____
WEEKS BEFORE BREAKING____

OCTOBER

DAYS BEFORE BREAKING_____
WEEKS BEFORE BREAKING____

NOVEMBER

DAYS BEFORE BREAKING_____
WEEKS BEFORE BREAKING____

DECEMBER

DAYS BEFORE BREAKING_____
WEEKS BEFORE BREAKING____

Long term financial planning requires an understanding of assets and liabilities. We are familiar with income and expenses because we need them to create monthly budgets. Unless we are accountants or financial analyst, assets and liabilities probably has little meaning. But, we need to know about them. They help us to understand the concept of net worth. A net worth of 0 or greater is the beginning of financial freedom. How do we measure our net worth? Compare all personal assets to all liabilities. An asset is anything owned that can be converted into cash. Some examples are properties, cash, automobiles, 401k accounts, IRA's, stock, and paintings. If an auto loan is greater than the value of the car; it is not an asset. If a house is less valuable than its mortgage loan, it isn't an asset. They are a liability. Liabilities are legally binding debts that must be paid. These are mortgages, auto loans, student loans, personal loans and other debts. It is easy to claim the ability to pay monthly expenses, but having a positive net worth is entirely different. What would happen if we were required to pay off all debts within 30 days? Most of us would panic and wonder about the consequences of non-payment. Those with positive net income would be more likely to pay their debts. This is how debt hinders our freedom. We are very vulnerable to the economy when we have more liabilities than assets. More than 50 percent of the United States has a negative net worth. After our monthly budgets are back in order we must plan to increase our net worth. To do this effectively we need to continually pay off debts and not create new debts. As our credit improves there will be more opportunities to increase debt. Marketers will throw the most enticing deals we have ever seen. Zero percent for 12 month. Get a brand new car with no money down. We will receive multiple advertisements targeted at our inner most desires. But, they will only slow down our progress. We must protect our net worth and never accept a debt that will create negative net worth.

SAMPLE PERSONAL BALANCE SHEET

Summary of Investments
Cash $
Fixed Income $
Equities $
Total Investment Assets $

Real Estate
Home Value $
Vacation Property $
Rental Property $
Limited Partnerships $
Other $
Total Real Estate $

Personal Assets
Jewelry $
Autos $
Furnishings $
Antiques $
Other $
Total Personal Assets $

Other Assets
Personal Loans Receivable $
Business Interests $
Other $
Total Other Assets $

Total Assets $

Liabilities
Home Mortgage $
Home Equity Loans $
Personal Loans $
Auto Loans$
Credit Card Balances $
Other Liabilities $
Total Liabilities $

Net Worth $

GETTING OUT OF DEBT

The journey towards financial freedom does not end once debt problems cease to exist. It is too easy to return to previous bad habits once some level of financial freedom is attained. Overcoming old debt problems can be equated to winning a battle, but the war will continue. Creditors will not stop marketing to promote debt growth. Retailers will continue to offer the most desired merchandise with options to postpone payments. Car salesman will try their best to convince potential buyers to replaced older vehicles with the latest models. Family members will continue to need financial assistance. Attractive people with the worst financial habits will be on the hunt for the financially stable. Debt temptations will be at an all-time high and walking away will not be easy. The best way to deal with this temptation is to accept the truth. Most people are attracted to reckless spending and relate this behavior to freedom. This attraction has developed over several decades and will not go away in one or two years. People often feel they aren't addicted to recklessness because they aren't making it rain in the club or going on frequent shopping sprees. People frequently assumed a lack of financial problems equates to being a consistently good money manager, but this is wrong. This disposition shows up in the most overlook instances. When we start serious relationships with financially incompatible people; we are being reckless. Recklessness shows up when we go out to nice restaurants and purchase an overly expensive bottle of wine. The moment we see an attractive pair of shoes but cannot resist the temptation to purchase a more expensive pair; recklessness has shown up. It was there when we were looking for a 55 inch flat screen television but grabbed a 65 inch instead. Reckless spending on small and large levels make us feel wealthy. We yearn for just a small taste of the wealth and will spend our money to fulfill this desire. Look at what happens to many lottery winners. They receive a large influx of cash and within a few years are filing bankruptcy. Based on recent studies, the likelihood of filing bankruptcy in 5 years is the same for $10,000 winners and $150,000 winners. Many of us feel this would not happen if we won the lottery, but I beg to differ. Money doesn't make a person a better money manager, but it does create more opportunities to increase debts. How often do we hear a story from the media about a celebrity filing for bankruptcy or having a home foreclose? In 2011 a short list of celebrities that have experienced these hardships would in include names like Chris Tucker, Burt Reynolds, Nadya Suleman (Ocotomom), Toni Braxton, Nicolas Cage, Latoya Jackson, Timothy Busfield, Rick Derringer, Teresa Giudice, Erin Moran, Carnie Wilson, Julius "Dr. J." Erving, Sergei Fedorov, Mel Gibson, Antoine Walker, Chamillionaire (Rapper), Terrell Owens and Alexis Bellino. Many of these same celebrities can also trace their marital problems back to money problems. Wealth attracts people and having multiple sex partners is almost expected of celebrities. What is the more highly sought lifestyle; a wealthy married person or a wealthy single person? The honest answer is the lifestyle of a wealthy single person and their endless option of attractive mates. Many married people envy this lifestyle and their pursuit of it is a major contributor to end their marriage. Fighting against these temptations requires consistent financial discipline and a high regard for marriage. Building this level of financial discipline doesn't happen overnight. It must become a lifestyle. This doesn't mean every decision should be financially beneficial, but it is important to understand when it should be considered.

14

EMPOWERING OTHERS

O ur country is engulfed in a debt culture and it affects everyone in the United States. There are no exemptions based on class, race, sexuality or gender. We witnessed what a society with a strong dependency of debt does to a country. It contributed to the creation of social class, hate, crime and the breakdown of strong communities. Debt has broken up families and shortens the dreams of our children. To get a true understanding of how debt affects our communities, we can look at recent news headlines. Home prices continue to fall. The unemployment rate continues to be above 8 percent and that's not accounting for any possible manipulation. Black Americans represent the highest unemployment rate. More than 50 percent of the country is receiving some form of public assistance. College graduates are not able to find jobs. They are also struggling to pay down their student debt. Crimes rates also indicate our country has a debt problem. Robbery, theft, murder, tax evasion, drug distribution, Ponzi schemes and other blue collar crimes are easily traced back to financial problems. Many people in our prisons lost their freedom in a direct response to their financial woes. Television producers may want us to believe all crimes are committed based on some deep evil trait, but reality is far different. Sitting in a few court sessions can really provide us with good perspectives. They can help us truly understand the root of many crimes. We would hear stories of murder based on unpaid debts or insurance claims. We would witness prosecutors build cases based on motives of financial gain. Witnesses would testify of instances where the accused needed money and seemed to be experiencing extreme financial hardships. Emails and tapped phone calls would reveal conversations about financial rewards as a result of committing a crime. Stories would be told about how being fired lead to thoughtless acts. We would hear defendants explaining how their inability to pay for traffic tickets, insurance coverage and registration expenses lead to driving without valid registration. Even the most polarizing trials of celebrities can often be traced back to money. The entire prosecution of Dr. Conrad Murray was based on choosing financial rewards over performing duties as a physician. O.J. Simpson may have beaten criminal charges for the murder of Nicole Simpson, but was later found guilty of robbery. The Menendez brothers were convicted for murdering their parents based on a motive of financial gain. Martha Stewart, Wesley Snipes, Bernie Madoff and Winona Ryder were all convicted of financial crimes. Time and time again we find financial motives behind criminal acts. This trend isn't anything new. What was the first crime many of us committed when we were children? The likely answer is some form of petty theft. It may have been stealing from another kid or the local corner store, but this type of act is very common. The motive goes back to wanting something we can't afford to get ourselves. There are some people with an addiction to stealing, but they are a minority. Wherever we find high rates of debt we will find high crime rates.

What happens when crime rates are high in any community? First the wealthy residents leave. They feel no need to stay when their property value will decrease and the threat of being robbed has increased. The remaining wealthy citizens usually find pockets within the community to isolate themselves. Next, some businesses close and relocate to safer more profitable areas. Small businesses also close due to a lack of profits and the threat of burglary. The remaining employers like Wal-Mart are usually not the best paying companies in the country. This results in a loss of jobs and a tougher job market. Overtime, good schools become average schools. The best teachers leave and donors also relocate. This contributes to less students graduating and children not being properly prepared for advancement. After seeing their parents struggle some children give in to the tempting offers of drug dealers. Parents also tend to lose sight of the actions of their children because of attention needed for finances. It can be pretty difficult for a child to turn down the instant gratification of drug money when their parents are struggling to provide for the household. There are some serious risks that accompany drug dealing, but many children figure this will be a short term situation. The risk is trumped by the reward. The government usually responds to this slow digression by increasing public assistance and implementing stronger policing tactics. They also try their best to attract business owners back to the community, but are being beaten out by less risky communities. These events combined with other factors destroy communities and they are difficult to rebuild.

Broken families also contribute to the fall of strong communities. While it is possible to raise successful families in single family homes, it is more difficult when compared to the opposite. One reason for the breakdown of many of these families is debt problems. Financial disputes are a leading cause of divorce in America. The end result of this expansion of debt is a wider separation of people based on income. Some people would even refer to this as class warfare. This is what breaks down nations and weaken communities. If we continue on this path of debt consumption then we will not continue to be known as a world leader. But, there is a way to get off this path.

We must empower each other to make better financial choices. We can do this by offering everyone an equal opportunity to learn how to overcome debt. I believe once we are given the information needed to make better choices, we will make better choices. Sure, some people prefer to be consumed by debt, but I want to believe this group is a minority. Most of us don't purposely become consumed by debt and must be taught to value financial freedom. This process will never happen overnight, but it is possible to arm people with the knowledge needed to defeat debt. First we must all accept one belief. We are only as strong as our weakest citizens.

When our neighbor losses their home then our property losses value. When our children are not being taught properly it affects the entire school. When people live their lives based on paying back debts then less people are truly able to enjoy life. Spreading the message of less debt consumption will help everyone and there are two tools we can to our advantage. These tools are communication and influence. The best way to influence others to consume less debt is to do it ourselves. We may not have the opportunity to effectively teach someone good financial principles, but we can certainly show them through our lives. Other people notice our actions and the joys of financial freedom are hard for anyone to ignore. They will want to know how we became so happy and what can be done to feel this way. They will also notice our failures. We must practice what we preach. How can we be an advocate for financial freedom if we are consistently making bad financial decisions? This is why it is so important to incorporate the financial lessons we learn into our lifestyle. Inconsistency lessens the impact of influence. The best place to begin spreading influence is within our households and families. We must prove celebrity idols are entertainers and not teachers. Our spouses must believe avoiding debt will lead to a better lifestyle. People within our households may not say it, but they are always judging our actions. Any parent will tell you their spouse or children are the first people to point out mistakes. Family members outside of our households also pay attention. They are even harder to share new ideas with if we seem inconsistent. How seriously would we consider the drinking advice from an alcoholic sibling? The other people we can impacts are our co-workers. The people we work with usually have an idea of how much money we make. This knowledge allows them to gain a slight understanding of our financial capabilities. They also pay attention to those complaining about not being paid enough and arguing with bill collectors. People living a financially free lifestyle usually don't display these actions. A positive attitude accompanies financial freedom and co-workers will want to know why we are so upbeat. This will present an opportunity to share and spread the message of financial freedom. People we come in contact with everyday are not the only people we can help.

The increased popularity of the internet allows us to reach thousands of people every day. We spend hours on the internet in search of stories, information and good conversations. People I come in contact with spend at least 3 hours per day on the internet. Social networking sites like Facebook and Twitter are seeing great profits even while our economy isn't doing well. YouTube has become the normal medium to share videos and spread ideas. Short Documentaries like KONY 2012 has been viewed over 80 million times on YouTube. The producers of this documentary were able to spread their message to millions using a free video sharing website. This would've cost million just a decade ago. Even national news broadcasters report on the latest viral video and celebrity tweets. We live in an era unlike any other before and it is our duty to use this tool. Getting millions of people to watch our videos may be unrealistic, but reaching 10 or 20 people is great. Fear of sounding silly or foolish can't be used as an excuse to not share this good news. All we need to do is share the story of how we overcame this debt culture. We don't need to be subject matter experts or great speakers. Sharing personal debt reduction stories in our own words will be enough. If uploading videos is too much work then adding insight to a blog can be useful. It doesn't take much effort to add an anonymous opinion to any political or financial blog. If we don't want to share our personal experiences; we can suggest a good book or helpful video. These blogs are also a good opportunity to learn new tips or insight leading to improved spending habits. We are never complete experts and can always learn more. The goal is to close the large gap between wealthy and poor Americans. Politicians can't create legislation that will fix this problem. Large corporations will not offer enough jobs to fix this problem. Police officers can't arrest people to fix this problem. We must fix this nationwide debt problem ourselves.

Imagine a country where the poorest citizens represent less than 1 percent of the total population. This country would be the most powerful, peaceful and influential nation in the world. This nation would avoid the failures of previous great nations because of the strength of its citizens. These people would be able to weather any recession that comes their way. Gas prices could double and these citizens would not miss a meal. They would have the ability to help themselves through difficult times. The worst criminals amongst them would be easier to capture because of the lack of criminal activity. Less people would suffer from depression and embrace the joys of life. New ideas and problem solving inventions would lead to consistent technological advancements. Other nations would look to this country for answers to their biggest problems. Its leaders would be forced to created meaningful legislation instead of playing politics. People would retire at an earlier age and pass less debt down to their children. Mistakes form the past which caused racial and social division would be forgiven. The children of this country would be highly educated and leaders amongst their peers worldwide. Their armed forces would also be more powerful than any other nation. This military has something many other nations don't; countless volunteers. What person wouldn't want to defend a country that provides such a prosperous lifestyle? I'm sure he or she would be a minority amongst these citizens. Most people are willing to defend a nation with so much promise. This may sound like a fairy tale but it could be reality. History has proven great change can occur when people come together. Why did we stop wilting to the rule of the British? A group of people decided they were tired of paying taxes to the Queen. Why was slavery outlawed in this country? American citizens forced a president to change the law. Who fought the government to make sure all people receive equal rights under the constitution? It wasn't most politicians. The people that were thrown in jail were normal American citizens. Who practiced civil disobedience to ensure women had a right to vote and receive equal pay? The most important changes happen because citizens want it to. This power has always belonged to the people and not governments. This power makes it possible for financial freedom to become reality. Today, this country revolves around debt, but we can end this cycle. There may come a time when peaceful protest are needed, but not in the beginning. We may need to vote out all the enablers of this debt culture, but there is something else to be done first. First, we must commit to changing our ways. We must be willing to be uncomfortable and adapt to new ideas. We have to ignore the distractions on the journey towards financial freedom. We must think beyond today and focus on creating a better tomorrow. Our nation's vitality depends on this change and I will do my part to create this change. I pray you will too.

EMPOWERING OTHERS

JANUARY BUDGET

MONTHLY INCOME
MONTHLY INCOME AFTER TAXES_____
MONTHLY INVESTMENT INCOME_____
MONTHLY INTEREST INCOME_____
TOTAL MONTHLY INCOME _____

MONTHLY EXPENSES

LOAN EXPENSES	**EDUCATION EXPENSES**
MORTGAGES_____	TUITION_____
AUTO LOANS_____	FEES_____
SCHOOL LOANS_____	SUPPLIES_____
PERSONAL LOANS_____	BOOKS_____
CREDIT CARDS_____	OTHER_____
TOTAL LOANS _____	**TOTAL EDUCATION** _____

SERVICE EXPENSES

GAS & ELECTRIC_____	HAIR/SKIN CARE_____
WATER_____	DAYCARE_____
TRASH PICKUP_____	BABYSITTING_____
SEWAGE REMOVAL_____	INTERNET _____
GYM MEMBERSHIP_____	SECURITY_____
FITNESS INSTRUCTION_____	DRY CLEANING_____
ATHLETIC INSTRUCTION_____	CABLE/SATELITE_____
MUSIC LESSONS_____	HOME CLEANING_____
ACTING LESSONS_____	CELL/TELEPHONE_____
CHILD RELATED LESSONS_____	AUTO MAINTINANCE_____
MAGAZINE/NEWSPAPER_____	OTHER_____

TOTAL SERVICE EXPENSES _____

MEDICAL EXPENSES	**TRANSPORTATION EXPENSES**
DENTAL_____	GAS_____
VISION_____	.PUBLIC TRANS_____
MEDICAL_____	INSURANCE_____
THERAPUDIC_____	TOLLS_____
COSMETIC_____	RENTAL_____
OTHER_____	OTHER_____
TOTAL MEDICAL _____	**TOTAL TRANS** _____

FOOD/HOME EXPENSES	**CLOTHING/LEISURE EXPENSES**
GROCERIES_____.	CLOTHES SHOPPING_____
FAST FOOD_____	OTHER SHOPPING _____
FARMING_____	DATING_____
HOME INSURANCE_____	VACATIONS_____
OTHER_____	OTHER_____
TOTAL FOOD/HOME _____	**TOTAL** _____

TOTAL ALL EXPENSES _____ **TOTAL ALL INCOME** _____

151

FEBRUARY BUDGET

MONTHLY INCOME
MONTHLY INCOME AFTER TAXES_____
MONTHLY INVESTMENT INCOME_____
MONTHLY INTEREST INCOME_____
TOTAL MONTHLY INCOME_____

MONTHLY EXPENSES

LOAN EXPENSES	EDUCATION EXPENSES
MORTGAGES_____	TUITION_____
AUTO LOANS_____	FEES_____
SCHOOL LOANS_____	SUPPLIES_____
PERSONAL LOANS_____	BOOKS_____
CREDIT CARDS_____	OTHER_____
TOTAL LOANS_____	**TOTAL EDUCATION**_____

SERVICE EXPENSES

GAS & ELECTRIC_____	HAIR/SKIN CARE_____
WATER_____	DAYCARE_____
TRASH PICKUP_____	BABYSITTING_____
SEWAGE REMOVAL_____	INTERNET _____
GYM MEMBERSHIP_____	SECURITY_____
FITNESS INSTRUCTION_____	DRY CLEANING_____
ATHLETIC INSTRUCTION_____	CABLE/SATELITE_____
MUSIC LESSONS_____	HOME CLEANING_____
ACTING LESSONS_____	CELL/TELEPHONE_____
CHILD RELATED LESSONS_____	AUTO MAINTINANCE_____
MAGAZINE/NEWSPAPER_____	OTHER_____

TOTAL SERVICE EXPENSES_____

MEDICAL EXPENSES	TRANSPORTATION EXPENSES
DENTAL_____	GAS_____
VISION_____	.PUBLIC TRANS_____
MEDICAL_____	INSURANCE_____
THERAPUDIC_____	TOLLS_____
COSMETIC_____	RENTAL_____
OTHER_____	OTHER_____
TOTAL MEDICAL_____	**TOTAL TRANS**_____

FOOD/HOME EXPENSES	CLOTHING/LEISURE EXPENSES
GROCERIES_____.	CLOTHES SHOPPING_____
FAST FOOD_____	OTHER SHOPPING _____
FARMING_____	DATING_____
HOME INSURANCE_____	VACATIONS_____
OTHER_____	OTHER_____
TOTAL FOOD/HOME_____	**TOTAL**_____
TOTAL ALL EXPENSES_____	**TOTAL ALL INCOME**_____

MARCH BUDGET

MONTHLY INCOME
MONTHLY INCOME AFTER TAXES_____
MONTHLY INVESTMENT INCOME_____
MONTHLY INTEREST INCOME_____
TOTAL MONTHLY INCOME_____

MONTHLY EXPENSES

LOAN EXPENSES	**EDUCATION EXPENSES**
MORTGAGES_____	TUITION_____
AUTO LOANS_____	FEES_____
SCHOOL LOANS_____	SUPPLIES_____
PERSONAL LOANS_____	BOOKS_____
CREDIT CARDS_____	OTHER_____
TOTAL LOANS	**TOTAL EDUCATION**

SERVICE EXPENSES

GAS & ELECTRIC_____	HAIR/SKIN CARE_____
WATER_____	DAYCARE_____
TRASH PICKUP_____	BABYSITTING_____
SEWAGE REMOVAL_____	INTERNET _____
GYM MEMBERSHIP_____	SECURITY_____
FITNESS INSTRUCTION_____	DRY CLEANING_____
ATHLETIC INSTRUCTION_____	CABLE/SATELITE_____
MUSIC LESSONS_____	HOME CLEANING_____
ACTING LESSONS_____	CELL/TELEPHONE_____
CHILD RELATED LESSONS_____	AUTO MAINTINANCE_____
MAGAZINE/NEWSPAPER_____	OTHER_____

TOTAL SERVICE EXPENSES

MEDICAL EXPENSES	**TRANSPORTATION EXPENSES**
DENTAL_____	GAS_____
VISION_____	.PUBLIC TRANS_____
MEDICAL_____	INSURANCE_____
THERAPUDIC_____	TOLLS_____
COSMETIC_____	RENTAL_____
OTHER_____	OTHER_____
TOTAL MEDICAL	**TOTAL TRANS**

FOOD/HOME EXPENSES	**CLOTHING/LEISURE EXPENSES**
GROCERIES_____.	CLOTHES SHOPPING_____
FAST FOOD_____	OTHER SHOPPING _____
FARMING_____	DATING_____
HOME INSURANCE_____	VACATIONS_____
OTHER_____	OTHER_____
TOTAL FOOD/HOME_____	**TOTAL**_____
TOTAL ALL EXPENSES_____	**TOTAL ALL INCOME**_____

APRIL BUDGET

MONTHLY INCOME
MONTHLY INCOME AFTER TAXES_____
MONTHLY INVESTMENT INCOME_____
MONTHLY INTEREST INCOME_____
TOTAL MONTHLY INCOME_____

MONTHLY EXPENSES

LOAN EXPENSES	**EDUCATION EXPENSES**
MORTGAGES_____	TUITION_____
AUTO LOANS_____	FEES_____
SCHOOL LOANS_____	SUPPLIES_____
PERSONAL LOANS_____	BOOKS_____
CREDIT CARDS_____	OTHER_____
TOTAL LOANS_____	**TOTAL EDUCATION**_____

SERVICE EXPENSES

GAS & ELECTRIC_____	HAIR/SKIN CARE_____
WATER_____	DAYCARE_____
TRASH PICKUP_____	BABYSITTING_____
SEWAGE REMOVAL_____	INTERNET_____
GYM MEMBERSHIP_____	SECURITY_____
FITNESS INSTRUCTION_____	DRY CLEANING_____
ATHLETIC INSTRUCTION_____	CABLE/SATELITE_____
MUSIC LESSONS_____	HOME CLEANING_____
ACTING LESSONS_____	CELL/TELEPHONE_____
CHILD RELATED LESSONS_____	AUTO MAINTINANCE_____
MAGAZINE/NEWSPAPER_____	OTHER_____

TOTAL SERVICE EXPENSES_____

MEDICAL EXPENSES	**TRANSPORTATION EXPENSES**
DENTAL_____	GAS_____
VISION_____	.PUBLIC TRANS_____
MEDICAL_____	INSURANCE_____
THERAPUDIC_____	TOLLS_____
COSMETIC_____	RENTAL _____
OTHER_____	OTHER_____
TOTAL MEDICAL_____	**TOTAL TRANS**_____

FOOD/HOME EXPENSES	**CLOTHING/LEISURE EXPENSES**
GROCERIES_____.	CLOTHES SHOPPING_____
FAST FOOD_____	OTHER SHOPPING _____
FARMING_____	DATING_____
HOME INSURANCE_____	VACATIONS_____
OTHER_____	OTHER_____
TOTAL FOOD/HOME_____	**TOTAL**_____
TOTAL ALL EXPENSES_____	**TOTAL ALL INCOME**_____

MONTHLY INCOME
MONTHLY INCOME AFTER TAXES_____
MONTHLY INVESTMENT INCOME_____
MONTHLY INTEREST INCOME_____
TOTAL MONTHLY INCOME_____

MONTHLY EXPENSES

LOAN EXPENSES

MORTGAGES_____
AUTO LOANS_____
SCHOOL LOANS_____
PERSONAL LOANS_____
CREDIT CARDS_____
TOTAL LOANS

EDUCATION EXPENSES

TUITION_____
FEES_____
SUPPLIES_____
BOOKS_____
OTHER_____
TOTAL EDUCATION

SERVICE EXPENSES

GAS & ELECTRIC_____
WATER_____
TRASH PICKUP_____
SEWAGE REMOVAL_____
GYM MEMBERSHIP_____
FITNESS INSTRUCTION_____
ATHLETIC INSTRUCTION_____
MUSIC LESSONS_____
ACTING LESSONS_____
CHILD RELATED LESSONS_____
MAGAZINE/NEWSPAPER_____

HAIR/SKIN CARE_____
DAYCARE_____
BABYSITTING_____
INTERNET _____
SECURITY_____
DRY CLEANING_____
CABLE/SATELITE_____
HOME CLEANING_____
CELL/TELEPHONE_____
AUTO MAINTINANCE_____
OTHER_____

TOTAL SERVICE EXPENSES_____

MEDICAL EXPENSES

DENTAL_____
VISION_____
MEDICAL_____
THERAPUDIC_____
COSMETIC_____
OTHER_____
TOTAL MEDICAL

TRANSPORTATION EXPENSES

GAS_____
.PUBLIC TRANS_____
INSURANCE_____
TOLLS_____
RENTAL_____
OTHER_____
TOTAL TRANS

FOOD/HOME EXPENSES

GROCERIES_____.
FAST FOOD_____
FARMING_____
HOME INSURANCE_____
OTHER_____
TOTAL FOOD/HOME_____

CLOTHING/LEISURE EXPENSES

CLOTHES SHOPPING_____
OTHER SHOPPING _____
DATING_____
VACATIONS_____
OTHER_____
TOTAL_____

TOTAL ALL EXPENSES_____**TOTAL ALL INCOME**_____

JUNE BUDGET

MONTHLY INCOME
MONTHLY INCOME AFTER TAXES_____
MONTHLY INVESTMENT INCOME_____
MONTHLY INTEREST INCOME_____
TOTAL MONTHLY INCOME_____

MONTHLY EXPENSES

LOAN EXPENSES   **EDUCATION EXPENSES**
MORTGAGES_____   TUITION_____
AUTO LOANS_____   FEES_____
SCHOOL LOANS_____   SUPPLIES_____
PERSONAL LOANS_____   BOOKS_____
CREDIT CARDS_____   OTHER_____
TOTAL LOANS_____   **TOTAL EDUCATION**_____

SERVICE EXPENSES
GAS & ELECTRIC_____   HAIR/SKIN CARE_____
WATER_____   DAYCARE_____
TRASH PICKUP_____   BABYSITTING_____
SEWAGE REMOVAL_____   INTERNET _____
GYM MEMBERSHIP_____   SECURITY_____
FITNESS INSTRUCTION_____   DRY CLEANING_____
ATHLETIC INSTRUCTION_____   CABLE/SATELITE_____
MUSIC LESSONS_____   HOME CLEANING_____
ACTING LESSONS_____   CELL/TELEPHONE_____
CHILD RELATED LESSONS_____ AUTO MAINTINANCE_____
MAGAZINE/NEWSPAPER_____   OTHER_____
TOTAL SERVICE EXPENSES_____

MEDICAL EXPENSES   **TRANSPORTATION EXPENSES**
DENTAL_____   GAS_____
VISION_____   .PUBLIC TRANS_____
MEDICAL_____   INSURANCE_____
THERAPUDIC_____   TOLLS_____
COSMETIC_____   RENTAL_____
OTHER_____   OTHER_____
TOTAL MEDICAL_____   **TOTAL TRANS**_____

FOOD/HOME EXPENSES   **CLOTHING/LEISURE EXPENSES**
GROCERIES_____.   CLOTHES SHOPPING_____
FAST FOOD_____   OTHER SHOPPING _____
FARMING_____   DATING_____
HOME INSURANCE_____   VACATIONS_____
OTHER_____   OTHER_____
TOTAL FOOD/HOME_____   **TOTAL**_____
TOTAL ALL EXPENSES_____   **TOTAL ALL INCOME**_____

JULY BUDGET

MONTHLY INCOME
MONTHLY INCOME AFTER TAXES_____
MONTHLY INVESTMENT INCOME_____
MONTHLY INTEREST INCOME_____
TOTAL MONTHLY INCOME_____

MONTHLY EXPENSES

LOAN EXPENSES	**EDUCATION EXPENSES**
MORTGAGES_____	TUITION_____
AUTO LOANS_____	FEES_____
SCHOOL LOANS_____	SUPPLIES_____
PERSONAL LOANS_____	BOOKS_____
CREDIT CARDS_____	OTHER_____
TOTAL LOANS	**TOTAL EDUCATION**

SERVICE EXPENSES

GAS & ELECTRIC_____	HAIR/SKIN CARE_____
WATER_____	DAYCARE_____
TRASH PICKUP_____	BABYSITTING_____
SEWAGE REMOVAL_____	INTERNET _____
GYM MEMBERSHIP_____	SECURITY_____
FITNESS INSTRUCTION_____	DRY CLEANING_____
ATHLETIC INSTRUCTION_____	CABLE/SATELITE_____
MUSIC LESSONS_____	HOME CLEANING_____
ACTING LESSONS_____	CELL/TELEPHONE_____
CHILD RELATED LESSONS_____	AUTO MAINTINANCE_____
MAGAZINE/NEWSPAPER_____	OTHER_____

TOTAL SERVICE EXPENSES

MEDICAL EXPENSES	**TRANSPORTATION EXPENSES**
DENTAL_____	GAS_____
VISION_____	.PUBLIC TRANS_____
MEDICAL_____	INSURANCE_____
THERAPUDIC_____	TOLLS_____
COSMETIC_____	RENTAL_____
OTHER_____	OTHER_____
TOTAL MEDICAL	**TOTAL TRANS**

FOOD/HOME EXPENSES	**CLOTHING/LEISURE EXPENSES**
GROCERIES_____.	CLOTHES SHOPPING_____
FAST FOOD_____	OTHER SHOPPING _____
FARMING_____	DATING_____
HOME INSURANCE_____	VACATIONS_____
OTHER_____	OTHER_____
TOTAL FOOD/HOME_____	**TOTAL**_____

TOTAL ALL EXPENSES_____ **TOTAL ALL INCOME**_____

157

AUGUST BUDGET

MONTHLY INCOME
MONTHLY INCOME AFTER TAXES_____
MONTHLY INVESTMENT INCOME_____
MONTHLY INTEREST INCOME_____
TOTAL MONTHLY INCOME_____

MONTHLY EXPENSES

LOAN EXPENSES	**EDUCATION EXPENSES**
MORTGAGES_____	TUITION_____
AUTO LOANS_____	FEES_____
SCHOOL LOANS_____	SUPPLIES_____
PERSONAL LOANS_____	BOOKS_____
CREDIT CARDS_____	OTHER_____
TOTAL LOANS_____	**TOTAL EDUCATION**_____

SERVICE EXPENSES

GAS & ELECTRIC_____	HAIR/SKIN CARE_____
WATER_____	DAYCARE_____
TRASH PICKUP_____	BABYSITTING_____
SEWAGE REMOVAL_____	INTERNET _____
GYM MEMBERSHIP_____	SECURITY_____
FITNESS INSTRUCTION_____	DRY CLEANING_____
ATHLETIC INSTRUCTION_____	CABLE/SATELITE_____
MUSIC LESSONS_____	HOME CLEANING_____
ACTING LESSONS_____	CELL/TELEPHONE_____
CHILD RELATED LESSONS_____	AUTO MAINTINANCE_____
MAGAZINE/NEWSPAPER_____	OTHER_____

TOTAL SERVICE EXPENSES_____

MEDICAL EXPENSES	**TRANSPORTATION EXPENSES**
DENTAL_____	GAS_____
VISION_____	.PUBLIC TRANS_____
MEDICAL_____	INSURANCE_____
THERAPUDIC_____	TOLLS_____
COSMETIC_____	RENTAL_____
OTHER_____	OTHER_____
TOTAL MEDICAL_____	**TOTAL TRANS** _____

FOOD/HOME EXPENSES	**CLOTHING/LEISURE EXPENSES**
GROCERIES_____.	CLOTHES SHOPPING_____
FAST FOOD_____	OTHER SHOPPING _____
FARMING_____	DATING_____
HOME INSURANCE_____	VACATIONS_____
OTHER_____	OTHER_____
TOTAL FOOD/HOME_____	**TOTAL**_____
TOTAL ALL EXPENSES_____	**TOTAL ALL INCOME**_____

SEPTEMBER BUDGET

MONTHLY INCOME
MONTHLY INCOME AFTER TAXES_____
MONTHLY INVESTMENT INCOME_____
MONTHLY INTEREST INCOME_____
TOTAL MONTHLY INCOME_____

MONTHLY EXPENSES

LOAN EXPENSES	**EDUCATION EXPENSES**
MORTGAGES_____	TUITION_____
AUTO LOANS_____	FEES_____
SCHOOL LOANS_____	SUPPLIES_____
PERSONAL LOANS_____	BOOKS_____
CREDIT CARDS_____	OTHER_____
TOTAL LOANS_____	**TOTAL EDUCATION**_____

SERVICE EXPENSES

GAS & ELECTRIC_____	HAIR/SKIN CARE_____
WATER_____	DAYCARE_____
TRASH PICKUP_____	BABYSITTING_____
SEWAGE REMOVAL_____	INTERNET _____
GYM MEMBERSHIP_____	SECURITY_____
FITNESS INSTRUCTION_____	DRY CLEANING_____
ATHLETIC INSTRUCTION_____	CABLE/SATELITE_____
MUSIC LESSONS_____	HOME CLEANING_____
ACTING LESSONS_____	CELL/TELEPHONE_____
CHILD RELATED LESSONS_____	AUTO MAINTINANCE_____
MAGAZINE/NEWSPAPER_____	OTHER_____

TOTAL SERVICE EXPENSES_____

MEDICAL EXPENSES	**TRANSPORTATION EXPENSES**
DENTAL_____	GAS_____
VISION_____	.PUBLIC TRANS_____
MEDICAL_____	INSURANCE_____
THERAPUDIC_____	TOLLS_____
COSMETIC_____	RENTAL_____
OTHER_____	OTHER_____
TOTAL MEDICAL_____	**TOTAL TRANS** _____

FOOD/HOME EXPENSES	**CLOTHING/LEISURE EXPENSES**
GROCERIES_____.	CLOTHES SHOPPING_____
FAST FOOD_____	OTHER SHOPPING _____
FARMING_____	DATING_____
HOME INSURANCE_____	VACATIONS_____
OTHER_____	OTHER_____
TOTAL FOOD/HOME_____	**TOTAL**_____
TOTAL ALL EXPENSES_____	**TOTAL ALL INCOME**_____

OCTOBER BUDGET

MONTHLY INCOME
MONTHLY INCOME AFTER TAXES_____
MONTHLY INVESTMENT INCOME_____
MONTHLY INTEREST INCOME_____
TOTAL MONTHLY INCOME_____

MONTHLY EXPENSES

LOAN EXPENSES	**EDUCATION EXPENSES**
MORTGAGES_____	TUITION_____
AUTO LOANS_____	FEES_____
SCHOOL LOANS_____	SUPPLIES_____
PERSONAL LOANS_____	BOOKS_____
CREDIT CARDS_____	OTHER_____
TOTAL LOANS_____	**TOTAL EDUCATION**_____

SERVICE EXPENSES

GAS & ELECTRIC_____	HAIR/SKIN CARE_____
WATER_____	DAYCARE_____
TRASH PICKUP_____	BABYSITTING_____
SEWAGE REMOVAL_____	INTERNET_____
GYM MEMBERSHIP_____	SECURITY_____
FITNESS INSTRUCTION_____	DRY CLEANING_____
ATHLETIC INSTRUCTION_____	CABLE/SATELITE_____
MUSIC LESSONS_____	HOME CLEANING_____
ACTING LESSONS_____	CELL/TELEPHONE_____
CHILD RELATED LESSONS_____	AUTO MAINTINANCE_____
MAGAZINE/NEWSPAPER_____	OTHER_____

TOTAL SERVICE EXPENSES_____

MEDICAL EXPENSES	**TRANSPORTATION EXPENSES**
DENTAL_____	GAS_____
VISION_____	.PUBLIC TRANS_____
MEDICAL_____	INSURANCE_____
THERAPUDIC_____	TOLLS_____
COSMETIC_____	RENTAL_____
OTHER_____	OTHER_____
TOTAL MEDICAL_____	**TOTAL TRANS**_____

FOOD/HOME EXPENSES	**CLOTHING/LEISURE EXPENSES**
GROCERIES_____.	CLOTHES SHOPPING_____
FAST FOOD_____	OTHER SHOPPING_____
FARMING_____	DATING_____
HOME INSURANCE_____	VACATIONS_____
OTHER_____	OTHER_____
TOTAL FOOD/HOME_____	**TOTAL**_____
TOTAL ALL EXPENSES_____	**TOTAL ALL INCOME**_____

NOVEMBER BUDGET

MONTHLY INCOME
MONTHLY INCOME AFTER TAXES_____
MONTHLY INVESTMENT INCOME_____
MONTHLY INTEREST INCOME_____
TOTAL MONTHLY INCOME_____

MONTHLY EXPENSES

LOAN EXPENSES	**EDUCATION EXPENSES**
MORTGAGES_____	TUITION_____
AUTO LOANS_____	FEES_____
SCHOOL LOANS_____	SUPPLIES_____
PERSONAL LOANS_____	BOOKS_____
CREDIT CARDS_____	OTHER_____
TOTAL LOANS_____	**TOTAL EDUCATION**_____

SERVICE EXPENSES

GAS & ELECTRIC_____   HAIR/SKIN CARE_____
WATER_____   DAYCARE_____
TRASH PICKUP_____   BABYSITTING_____
SEWAGE REMOVAL_____   INTERNET _____
GYM MEMBERSHIP_____   SECURITY_____
FITNESS INSTRUCTION_____   DRY CLEANING_____
ATHLETIC INSTRUCTION_____   CABLE/SATELITE_____
MUSIC LESSONS_____   HOME CLEANING_____
ACTING LESSONS_____   CELL/TELEPHONE_____
CHILD RELATED LESSONS_____   AUTO MAINTINANCE_____
MAGAZINE/NEWSPAPER_____   OTHER_____
TOTAL SERVICE EXPENSES_____

MEDICAL EXPENSES	**TRANSPORTATION EXPENSES**
DENTAL_____	GAS_____
VISION_____	.PUBLIC TRANS_____
MEDICAL_____	INSURANCE_____
THERAPUDIC_____	TOLLS_____
COSMETIC_____	RENTAL_____
OTHER_____	OTHER_____
TOTAL MEDICAL_____	**TOTAL TRANS**_____

FOOD/HOME EXPENSES	**CLOTHING/LEISURE EXPENSES**
GROCERIES_____.	CLOTHES SHOPPING_____
FAST FOOD_____	OTHER SHOPPING _____
FARMING_____	DATING_____
HOME INSURANCE_____	VACATIONS_____
OTHER_____	OTHER_____
TOTAL FOOD/HOME_____	**TOTAL**_____
TOTAL ALL EXPENSES_____	**TOTAL ALL INCOME**_____

161

DECEMBER BUDGET

MONTHLY INCOME
MONTHLY INCOME AFTER TAXES_____
MONTHLY INVESTMENT INCOME_____
MONTHLY INTEREST INCOME_____
TOTAL MONTHLY INCOME_____

MONTHLY EXPENSES

LOAN EXPENSES	**EDUCATION EXPENSES**
MORTGAGES_____	TUITION_____
AUTO LOANS_____	FEES_____
SCHOOL LOANS_____	SUPPLIES_____
PERSONAL LOANS_____	BOOKS_____
CREDIT CARDS_____	OTHER_____
TOTAL LOANS_____	**TOTAL EDUCATION_____**

SERVICE EXPENSES

GAS & ELECTRIC_____	HAIR/SKIN CARE_____
WATER_____	DAYCARE_____
TRASH PICKUP_____	BABYSITTING_____
SEWAGE REMOVAL_____	INTERNET_____
GYM MEMBERSHIP_____	SECURITY_____
FITNESS INSTRUCTION_____	DRY CLEANING_____
ATHLETIC INSTRUCTION_____	CABLE/SATELITE_____
MUSIC LESSONS_____	HOME CLEANING_____
ACTING LESSONS_____	CELL/TELEPHONE_____
CHILD RELATED LESSONS_____	AUTO MAINTINANCE_____
MAGAZINE/NEWSPAPER_____	OTHER_____

TOTAL SERVICE EXPENSES_____

MEDICAL EXPENSES	**TRANSPORTATION EXPENSES**
DENTAL_____	GAS_____
VISION_____	.PUBLIC TRANS_____
MEDICAL_____	INSURANCE_____
THERAPUDIC_____	TOLLS_____
COSMETIC_____	RENTAL_____
OTHER_____	OTHER_____
TOTAL MEDICAL_____	**TOTAL TRANS_____**

FOOD/HOME EXPENSES	**CLOTHING/LEISURE EXPENSES**
GROCERIES_____.	CLOTHES SHOPPING_____
FAST FOOD_____	OTHER SHOPPING_____
FARMING_____	DATING_____
HOME INSURANCE_____	VACATIONS_____
OTHER_____	OTHER_____
TOTAL FOOD/HOME_____	**TOTAL_____**
TOTAL ALL EXPENSES_____	**TOTAL ALL INCOME_____**

About the Author

Joseph Lorick was born August 25th 1981 in Baltimore, MD. He graduated from the 3rd oldest high school in the country, Baltimore City College, in 1999. He went on to earn his bachelors in business administration from Bowie State University. As a senior, Joseph began his career in banking and has never stopped. He has worked in the Collections, Credit, Mortgage, Consumer Loans, Consumer Checking, Small Business Checking and Strategies department within his 9 years of employment. During this time, he has spoken with thousands of customers and gained extensive knowledge about the financial habits of American citizens. Joseph is also a Christian and has been for the last 18 years. He works in the church as a financial counselor and also serves as a worship coordinator. During his spare time he leads financial freedom lectures and assists his community by teaching financial literacy. He is a strong believer in social progression through education and writes to further this cause. Above all professional responsibilities; Joseph considers being a husband his most important role.

To receive daily debt tips and other helpful financial advice follow Joseph Lorick on Twitter @DidEvthButThink or on Facebook.

D.E.B.T. Volume 2 coming soon!

D.E.B.T.S. "Did Everything But Think Spiritually" coming soon!

Thanks
Shon